A Primal Issue

Jagadish Gupta was a Bengali writer and pioneer of the modernist movement in the 1920s. He published eight novels, eight short story collections, and some poetry, and his writing took Bengal's literary world by storm. He earned both praise and criticism from Rabindranath Tagore, which brought him much critical attention. Born in 1886, he worked a number of smaller jobs before finally quitting to concentrate primarily on his literary career, until his death in 1957. Some of his works include *Binodini* (1927), *Laghu-Guru* (1931) and *Akshara* (1932).

Subrata Basu lives in Kolkata, writes in English and Bengali, and translates both ways between these languages. His translations have been published by the Sahitya Akademi, National Book Trust and a leading publisher of Kolkata. He was awarded First Prize in 2007 in the Oral Literature division of an all-India literary translation competition held by the Sahitya Akademi. He takes an interest, midway between a layman's and an academic's, in science, literature and the history of Soviet Communism.

A Primal Issue

Stories of Women

JAGADISH GUPTA

Translated from the original Bengali by

SUBRATA BASU

Orient BlackSwan

A PRIMAL ISSUE: STORIES OF WOMEN

ORIENT BLACKSWAN PRIVATE LIMITED

Registered Office
3-6-752 Himayatnagar, Hyderabad 500 029, Telangana, India
e-mail: centraloffice@orientblackswan.com

Other Offices
Bengaluru, Bhopal, Chennai, Guwahati,
Hyderabad, Jaipur, Kolkata, Lucknow, Mumbai,
New Delhi, Noida, Patna, Visakhapatnam

First published by Orient Blackswan Private Limited 2020

ISBN 978-93-5287-904-5

030963

Typeset in
Amethyst 10.5/13.5
by Le Studio Graphique, Gurgaon 122 007

Printed in India at
Akash Press, Delhi

Published by
Orient Blackswan Private Limited
3-6-752, Himayatnagar, Hyderabad 500 029, Telangana, India
e-mail: info@orientblackswan.com

For
those who cannot read in Bengali
and
those who can but do not

Contents

Acknowledgements *ix*

Introduction *xi*
SUBRATA BASU

Note on Pronunciation *xxiii*

A Primal Issue 1

A Bond Defiled 20

So Long as the Sun and Moon 40

Son and Son's Wife 58

Krishna's Consummation 80

Mrs Havoc 97

The Eighteenth Art 107

Acknowledgements

It is deeply instructive that even a small volume such as this has to owe so much to so many.

I was able to track down the death certificate of Jagadish Gupta, thanks to a smart idea suggested by my wife Nalini. This alone resolved the copyright uncertainties which had kept this translation from being published for five years.

From the publishers' side, Madhavi Menon and Nilanjana Majumdar took crucial initiative at different points, and editor Noella James showed great understanding.

My daughter Smita, and Jaydeb Pathak of Ramgarh Colony, Kolkata, helped me locate and photograph the house in which Jagadish Gupta lived during his last years. The house does not exist anymore.

My daughter Shukti provided the ambience and, together with the others, the support that I needed at a very difficult time during the final preparation of the manuscript.

Introduction

Jagadish Gupta was a pioneer of the great modernist movement that, from the mid-1920s, began to radically transform Bengali fiction after its near-exclusive domination by Rabindranath Tagore and Saratchandra Chattopadhyay. He was arguably even *the* pioneer of this movement, having begun his literary career nearly a decade earlier than its much better-known exponent, Manik Bandyopadhyay. He published eight novels, eight short story collections, and some poetry, but it is generally agreed that his most significant contribution was his short stories.

Born in 1886 in the Kushtia district of present-day Bangladesh, Jagadish Gupta graduated from a Kolkata school in 1905, married Charubala in 1906, and entered college, but dropped out a year later. In 1908, he started working as a typist at a suburban law court. From then until 1944, except for a rather adventurous two years in between, this would be his profession. He worked as a jobbing typist, barring the years 1912–25, when he held a regular job. He resigned from this job, following a difference of opinion with his British superior over a capital letter, never to take up regular employment again. He then brought out a journal, carrying his own stories in each issue, which was not a great hit. Next, turning entrepreneur, he started manufacturing fountain pen ink under the brand name *Jago's Ink* (*Jago* obviously from Jagadish), but this, too, failed to catch on. Sobered by these experiences, he went back to his original trade of a jobbing typist in 1927 and concentrated on his literary career. For the rest of his life, undeterred by poverty, neglect and ill-health, he pursued his art and his unique vision of the world with fanatic devotion, disdaining to make any concessions to popular taste, unlike even the iconic Saratchandra Chattopadhyay or Tarashankar Bandyopadhyay. He read extensively in Western literature, making references to Shakespeare and Molière in his correspondence, and was a lover of music who also played several musical instruments. He lived the last seven years of his life with his wife in a settlement for refugees from East Pakistan (which is now Bangladesh) near Kolkata, where they, being childless, adopted and brought up a girl. In 1954, he was granted a monthly government pension of Rs 150, which was later reduced to Rs 75. Suffering a head injury from a fall, Jagadish Gupta died in a cousin's house in south Kolkata in 1957.[1]

C36 Ramgarh Colony, where Jagadish Gupta lived during his last years. Photographed in 2013 and since demolished, it was originally, and long afterwards, a bamboo structure on an earthen floor. Jagadish Gupta named it Bandhani, which has the double meaning of 'what binds' and 'what encloses'.

His first book, a collection of short stories, came out in 1927. These stories apparently earned a word of praise from Tagore for the "characteristic form and flavour of the short story" as well as the "new forms and flavours"[2] manifest in them. However, it is his first novel, *Laghu-Guru* (*The Light and the Serious*), about a prostitute, published four years later, that took Bengal's literary world by storm. He was then forty-five, a somewhat unlikely age for a rebel; and Tagore, whose pervasive influence the modernist movement was striving to overcome, was in the last decade of his life. Tagore wrote a review of the novel in the leading Bengali literary journal, *Porichoy*, in which he was as forthright in his criticism of the novel as he was in his recognition of the author's literary power:[3]

> I know absolutely nothing of the ways of the world that is described in this novel. Perhaps even the writer himself, quitting the highway in search of things not-too-familiar, went over across thorn-bushes and came back after taking a peek at that spot.
>
> The reason for this doubt of mine is that the writer has presented his case to us but has not been able to marshal adequate support for it. From this piece of writing at any rate, no signs are available that he has himself witnessed it all. [He] has simply taken it for granted that we of our own accord will come forward to accept it.
>
> One thing ought to be said. The story, it is true, is about social muck but there is no zest for muckraking in it. The appearance of the story does not give the impression of indubitable authenticity—herein lies my objection.
>
> Anyway, it has to be admitted that the author does have a flair for writing. He will suffer harm if the temptation to drum up on the cheap a gala show of *realism*[4] at modernist gatherings gets the better of him.

In a short story collection that followed the novel, Jagadish Gupta replied:

> Among the judgements passed by various people on my book, the [above] is the main. The reason is that its dispenser is Rabindranath himself; and the second reason is that it goes off the mark and misses the matter in question—that is to say, it attacks the innocent parent of the accused rather than the accused itself.
>
> The appearance of the concluding part of the book review, because of its uncivil sting, does not give the impression of a book review—herein lies my objection. The two words, 'not-too-familiar' and 'spot' are very *realistic* no doubt [but], while commuting, thanks to the faulty *town-planning* of Bolpur,[5] 'that spot' came into sight of itself; there was no need to take a peek.
>
> My objection is that while reviewing the book it would have been better not to refer to the biography of the writer.

It is, of course, not possible to take a stand in this dispute without considering the novel in question. But, strictly on the basis of the texts before us, we can clearly see that Jagadish Gupta's *response*, at any rate, was quite misplaced.

Tagore is saying that, in his opinion, the novel lacks the authenticity of direct experience, and this makes him wonder, somewhat cuttingly, no doubt, if the writer is really familiar with the things he has undertaken to depict. No matter whether Tagore's contention is sound or not, he cannot be accused of indulging in an uncivil personal attack. The remarkably detailed and searching analysis in fact seemed to suggest that he regarded this debut novel of a middle-aged writer as representative of the emerging trend in Bengali literature and, by way of this review, was expressing his views on this movement as a whole.

On the other hand, whatever be the merits of Jagadish Gupta's rejoinder to Tagore, it says something about the spine of a man who, bent over a typewriter for thirty-odd years for a living, produced writings that brought him neither popular success nor money.

And apparently, this same man dedicated his next collection of stories to Tagore using the traditional Bengali phrasing which, translated, would read: "At the hallowed feet of Srijukta Rabindranath Thakur".[6]

Today Jagadish Gupta is unanimously acclaimed by critics as one of the towering figures and a trailblazer of modernism in Bengali literature for his unsentimental, anti-romantic temper, his uncompromisingly analytical approach, his unflinching exploration of sexuality and of the dark, taboo areas of the mind, and his pitiless depiction of the sordid undercurrents of family and social life. On occasion, these preoccupations of his suddenly light up with a brilliant, earthy humour that is all his own. Yet, as far as general readers are concerned, he remains, quite unjustifiably, in relative obscurity.

For his time, and for a small-town scribbler, Jagadish Gupta appears to have been most improbably original in his approach, and almost absurdly stubborn in his artistic convictions. His iconoclasm, on the other hand, in sharp contrast to that of some of his younger fellow rebels,[7] is uncompromisingly home-grown; and his writings, though startlingly modern, are almost exclusively focused on rural or semi-rural life, and never flashy.

In addition, he has a highly individual style, which even his admirers have sometimes found demanding. Certainly, it is his very strength as a thoroughly indigenous modernist that has engendered many of his stylistic features: truncated sentences, tortuous syntax, complex and continual interplay of expression and suggestion, abundant use of local words and rustic turns of speech, etc. That apart, there is an inevitable tension between his audacious themes and the degree of frankness allowed by the literary conventions of his day, and his writings bear the imprint of his struggle to master this contradiction.

Such a combination of content and style was hardly a recipe for huge success with the general literary public of his day. But, far ahead of his time then, he is by the same token eminently capable of being more readily and widely appreciated today.

The themes and attitudes he introduced many decades ago in complete defiance of the conservative outcry of society can still enormously enrich our awareness of the human condition, and deeply affect the way we are accustomed to looking at our world.

It is therefore somewhat astonishing that this should be the first ever attempt to make a collection of writings of this daring innovator available to a readership outside Bengal. Still more astonishing is the fact that all his major writings are not available even in Bengal today.[8] Hopefully, this present effort in English will serve as a well-deserved reminder to Bengalis themselves of one of their great authors.

There is another expectation of a more fundamental nature from this collection: that it might help to bring about a long-due correction of an entrenched critical prejudice. While acknowledging the achievements of Jagadish Gupta, critics have also often accused him of an extremely one-sided pessimism and cynicism. How misplaced this accusation is becomes apparent in the very first story when, near the end of it, the man cries out, “It is all my fault, beat me, too”. In fact, all the stories in this book, which I am shortly going to outline, would eloquently argue against this unfair criticism.

Every translation is based on a certain interpretation of the original, which usually remains tacit. But it seems to me that the fact that a translation so often *feels* right or wrong without comparison with the original—most readers react to a translation without consulting the original anyway—is actually determined by this *underlying* interpretation. The primary purpose of the brief story outlines offered below is to make explicit, so far as possible in a limited space, my own interpretation, so that readers can readily decide to what extent this is responsible for the “feel” they get from reading these translations—especially if any of them does *not* feel quite right.

Besides, there is no great logic behind the arrangement of the stories in this collection, but mainly the translator’s personal preference. The outlines provided may help readers decide in what order they would like to read the stories.

One important point ought to be made here. As they go on to read this book, present-day readers may well wonder whether the protagonists in some of the stories are not implausibly young for the events they are shown to be involved in. If so, it will perhaps suffice to recall that Shakespeare's Juliet was all of fourteen years old at the time of her high tragedy. The truth is that when people were married off early, they matured, or were made to mature, early, too.

The first story, 'A Primal Issue', is about a young widow, Kanchan, who, in desperate need of male support and protection, marries her five-year-old daughter Khushi to twenty-four-year-old Subal. Subal's real target is, however, Kanchan herself and, for him, marrying Khushi is the only way of gaining access to her. Thus, the story brings together two brutal social realities—child marriage and the Hindu taboo on widow remarriage—that are at odds with the primal reality of human nature, and yet are not extinct even today. The consequence of this combination is then played out with the grimness of a Greek tragedy.

In the second story, 'A Bond Defiled', Satkari will come home after serving a prison term for rape. His doting mother waits anxiously; his brother is dutiful, though rather shamefaced; and only his brother's wife can truly feel what is going on in the mind of Satkari's wife, Makhanbala. The next day Satkari slips into the house in the evening under cover of darkness. His mother feeds him and fusses over him to her heart's content, and then orders Makhanbala into his bedroom. How Makhanbala faces her moment of truth forms the climax of the story.

The third story is 'So Long as the Sun and Moon'. Whether or not we like to remember it, polygamy is still alive in large parts of the world, and the fact that the co-wives in this story are sisters brings out the raw, everyday reality of the practice with searing vividness. Dinataran's wife, Kshanaprabha, has borne him a child that is eight months old when his parents marry him again, to her younger sister, and overnight Kshanaprabha is, as it were, quartered into wife, ex-wife, mother and sister. Immediately after this marriage, however, Dinataran's mother realises the wrong that has been done to Kshanaprabha and feels guilty. Attempting to make amends, she brings about the horrific ending of the story.

In the next story, 'Son and Son's Wife', Amrita has turned out to be the black sheep of the family and a social nuisance. To tempt him over to the straight and narrow, his father, Akshay, resorts to the time-honoured ploy of marrying him to a girl of surpassing beauty, Maya. Amrita, of course, persists in his old ways, causing Maya all kinds of indignities and making life hell for her. Finally, when one of Amrita's victims, a helpless woman of a lower caste, comes and reveals the full extent of his misdeeds, it proves the last straw for Maya and she goes back to her parents' house. Akshay is torn between his resentment at this affront and affection for his daughter-in-law. He eventually goes to bring her back but is met with refusal, which enrages him. However, his wife, belying the archetypal image of a mother-in-law, empathises with Maya.

The fifth story, 'Krishna's Consummation', must surely be one of the first in modern Indian literature to acknowledge not only lesbianism but, with breathtaking prevision and daring, a far greater fluidity of sexual orientation. Right from the age of ten, the precocious Ranu has been in love with the seventeen-year-old Kanu, the boy next door, but with typical male obtuseness, Kanu remains oblivious of this. When at last his own passion for her is roused, she has already been married off elsewhere and is beyond his reach. Years later, Ranu, with her family, becomes his next-door neighbour once again, but she pointedly ignores him while befriending his wife, Indira. When the time comes for Ranu's family to leave the town, Ranu asks to spend a night with Indira for a last chat. During the night Indira is surprised and amused by Ranu's love-making, but Kanu reads a different, deeper meaning in it.

The title of the next story, 'Mrs Havoc', is a reminder of how in India a woman is reviled as *pralayankari* or 'havoc-causing', while also being deified as an embodiment of the elemental, cosmic force. So, would not any such force, if misused, as women constantly are, cause havoc? The rich merchant Sodu Khan robs the poor Jasim of his young wife by fiendish cunning and naked force. Twenty-two poor, low-caste Hindus, rallying in support of the poor Muslim Jasim, confront two hundred hirelings of the rich Muslim Sodu Khan. What happens then? What happens to Jasim's wife?

The last story, 'The Eighteenth Art', is one of the relatively few humorous stories written by Jagadish Gupta. Janaki is a remarkably intelligent woman deeply in love with her simple-minded husband, Benukar. But Benukar is feeling jaded after four years of marriage. He wants some zest, fun and playfulness brought into their life by the 'arts' that he believes Janaki, as a woman, should possess. Janaki decides to teach him a lesson. She plants a live *magur* fish in the field Benukar is going to plough. Benukar duly finds the fish and the story builds up to its comic denouement. The humour is at the expense of Benukar, as well as the smug male in general, but remains gentle, warm and loving.

It will be seen from the outlines presented above that all the stories have women as their protagonists. This provides the collection with a unifying motif but, fortunately, not at the expense of scope. The entire range of his above-mentioned characteristics as a modernist writer in respect of both content and style is on display here.[9] Of course, these very characteristics—in particular, of his style—make Jagadish Gupta a singularly difficult author to translate. But his style is integral to his art, and can thus be an absorbing object of study in itself. I have therefore avoided simplifying or smartening him up, and have only permitted myself sometimes to join two paragraphs or break up one, alter the punctuation, and divide a story into more sections than there may have been in the original.

To my judgement, these departures from absolute literalness detract nothing of substance from the translation but contribute immensely to the reader's comprehension and comfort. Purists might frown, of course, but no translation theory will ever persuade me that the authenticity of a translation is to be judged by the hard time it manages to give the reader. In fact, more generally, how significant the numerous theories with their diverse prescriptions at all prove to be in *practice* is not clear to me. All too often the winning of appreciation by even a most talented writer outside his or her own language appears to depend far more on factors which are ultimately political and economic. And, moreover, the farther, culturally, the target language is from the original—in the sense that English is farther from Bengali than from, say, Spanish or Icelandic—the greater seems to be this dependence.[10]

Apart from the reading conveniences detailed above, my aim, naturally, has been to capture the distinctive flavour of Jagadish Gupta's Bengali prose as well as his individual tone, including even his mannerisms, occasional archaisms, rhetorical flourishes and verbal extravagance. This has made work excruciatingly slow and strenuous and has tested, quite severely, the elasticity of the English language as I know it. But it has been worth it. For in recent years, just as there have been translations from Bengali that are commendable in terms of both fidelity and readability, there have also been some that take appalling liberties with the greatest works of Bengali literature, sometimes loftily offering, as if in compensation, an Englishman's English, frequently not even that. This collection attempts to make a simple, unoriginal point: great authors of the past can be compellingly readable without any insolent editing. Jagadish Gupta is one such writer of the Bengali language.

Notes

1. For the biographical information summarised in this paragraph, I have found the best single source in *Jagadish Gupta* by Hiren Chattopadhyay (New Delhi: Sahitya Akademi, 2009). Some facts of

his life and career are available in numerous other sources such as Wikipedia, *Jagadish Guptar Galpa*, edited by Subir Raychaudhury (Kolkata: Dey's Publishing, 2004), and Akademi Vidyarthi Bangla Abhidhan (Kolkata: Paschimbanga Bangla Akademi, 2009). It has also been possible, after a gap of sixty years, to unearth his death certificate and check the date and place of his death with it. Some items in his death certificate are not filled in (simply marked 'N.M.', i.e. 'Not Mentioned'), such as his own address and, more notably, the name of his wife, who was alive. These omissions, no matter what they were actually due to, tend to darken our perception of his last days with a strong sense of forlornness.

2. These two quotations appear in *Jagadish Gupta* by Hiren Chattopadhyay (2009), and have been translated by me.

3. What follows is made up of excerpts, with ellipses dispensed with in order to lessen the reader's discomfort. Tagore's review was published in 1931 in *Porichoy*, Ist Year, 2nd Issue, pp. 314–17, available at sanhati.com/porichoy. I became aware of the review by reading quotations from it in *Jagadish Guptar Galpa*, edited by Subir Raychaudhuri (Kolkata: Dey's Publishing, 2004), and *Jagadish Gupta* by Hiren Chattopadhyay (New Delhi: Sahitya Akademi, 2009). Jagadish Gupta's response to the review, similarly excerpted here, is also quoted variously in both these books. All the excerpts have been translated by me.

4. The italics here and in the rest of these excerpts indicate English words that were used in the Bengali texts of Tagore and Jagadish Gupta.

5. Bolpur is the railway station that serves Tagore's Santiniketan, and the "spot" was obviously a brothel nearby. Although Jagadish Gupta spent a large part of his working life in Bolpur, I have not come across any evidence that he ever met Tagore.

6. In *Jagadish Guptar Galpa*, the editor, Subir Raychaudhuri, states that in the copy of this collection that he managed to trace, there was no dedication page, but on the first page, the dedication to Tagore was inscribed in Jagadish Gupta's own hand and signed by him.

7. These rebels belonged to the so-called '*Kallol* period' that unleashed the mighty tide of modernism in Bengali literature around the mid-1920s (*Kallol* means something like 'a resounding tide'). This period takes its name from *Kallol*, the first important magazine

to provide a platform for the avant-garde writers. Over time, a few other magazines of a similar persuasion, such as *Kaali O Kalam* (Pen and Ink), made their appearance. Jagadish Gupta contributed to both *Kallol* and *Kaali O Kalam*.

8. Photographs of him generally available are very few, too. One that is readily found on the Internet, but the copyright status of which is not clear, also appears in *Jagadish Guptar Galpa*, edited by Subir Raychaudhuri (Kolkata: Dey's Publishing, 2004), where it is attributed to Parimal Goswami, a renowned journalist and writer of the day and a photographer of note. The same image is used on the cover of *Jagadish Gupta* by Hiren Chattopadhyay (New Delhi: Sahitya Akademi, 2009).

9. However, he also wrote stories in which catastrophes are shown, unambiguously, to have a supernatural origin. How these stories square with his modernist vision may be an interesting point of debate, but there can be no two opinions that some of them—such as '*Dibaser Seshe*' ('At Day's End') and '*Haarh*' ('The Bone')—are remarkable feats of technical finesse and the sheer art of storytelling.

10. For instance, Tagore is arguably, if nothing else, one of the greatest songwriters of the world (in the opinion of some, like Satyajit Ray, he is *the* greatest). And yet, one can be pretty sure that, as long as the status of India in the world and that of Bengal in India remain what they are, no amount of translation and re-translation according to this or that theory will bring about a dramatic upswing in the appreciation of Tagore outside Bengal. Ergo, it is not merely (or at all) a question of replacing the 'thous' and the 'thees'. Of course, this is not to say that these efforts should not continue. Politico-economic status can change and, to complicate matters, it does not always have to change for the better for an arousal of interest! Meanwhile these efforts do serve to keep alive a tradition, eliciting some appreciation here and there.

Note on Pronunciation

Readers will not be inflicted with diacritics while reading the book. By and large, the Bengali words, mostly names, will be spelt the way Bengalis would usually spell them in English. The main thing to remember about them is that *s*, *i* and *u* are in general to be pronounced as *sh*, *ee*, and *oo*, respectively, and that *a* is not to be pronounced as in *ham*, but as the *o* in *hot* or *more* (the distinction is not terribly important for the present purpose), or as the *a* in *half*. Some instances where the spelling may still lead a reader too far away from the Bengali sound are listed below on the left, with their approximate pronunciations provided on the right:

Adi Kathar Ekti	Aadi Kathaar Ekti
Ahuti	Aahootee
Akshayananda	Akkhayaananda
Alta	Aaltaa
Amba	Ambaa
Amrita	Amrito
Arati	Aarotee
Aruper Ras	Arooper Raash
Atharo Kalar Ekti	Aathaaro Kalaar Ekti
Baman	Baamon
Basar	Baashor

Batasa	Baataashaa
Chandra Surya Jatadin	Chandro Soorjo Jatodeen
Gatihara Jahnabi	Gotihaaraa Janhobee
Harimati	Horeemotee
Jadugopal	Jodoogopaal
Janaki	Jaanokee
Kalankita Samparka	Kalankito Samaparko
Kali, Karali	Kaalee, Karaalee
Kalyani	Kol-laanee
Kshanaprabha	Khanoprobhaa
Makhanbala	Maakhonbaalaa
Pralayankari Shashthi	Proloyankoree Shoshthee
Putra Ebang Putrabadhu	Pootro Ebang Pootrobodhoo
Rai	Rye
Rudraksha	Roodraakkho
Satkari/Satu	Shaatkori/Shaatoo

A Primal Issue*

One day at midnight, Beni heard someone whisper from the other side of his hut's wicker[1]-wall: "Hari?" Two or three times. A male voice. And Harimati was the name of Beni's wife.

Pricking up his ears, Beni waited for a while, and then got out of his bed in utmost stealth and silence. Going on tiptoe, the moment he flung aside the bolt of the door with a bang, the man who was calling "Hari, Hari" ran off, crashing through bushes and thickets.

Beni did give chase but, unable to make out clearly in the dark, couldn't do much.

Coming back, Beni lit the lamp in the room. The big chopper was stuck into the wicker-wall. With one stroke of it he neatly lopped off the sleeping Harimati's head, and landed up straight at the police station in the dead of that very night, with the head and the glistening, blood-smeared chopper. In reply to police interrogation, Beni didn't conceal anything, or contradict anything. Till the end he stuck to his blunt confession of murder.

He is sentenced to hanging.

*Originally published in Bengali as '*Adi Kathar Ekti*', in 1929.

Such a big event comes to pass—for a most trivial reason, though. This was at the root of it.

The five Das families lived at one end of the village, but they were not ones to live in peace and quiet. Their young and old, men and women, would kick up such a hullabaloo and scramble for a mango or a *jaam* or a betel-nut or a *karamchaa* lying about under a tree, as if it was their only asset and they had been reduced to complete penury because so-and-so's son had picked it up and taken it home. A rumpus such as this perhaps would be in order if the ripe crop in one's paddy field was grazed clean by another's cows overnight. But no, this was simply a life-and-death feud: one could hack the other into pieces and eat him up, such was the vehemence.

Thus it had been going on all twelve months and thirty days. Only contests of shouting and cursing.

Beni Das was the terror of the neighbourhood; he was the most perverse, the most hot-tempered, as well as the burliest of all. Unable to get the better of him in brawls, his own relatives, kinsmen and neighbours had hatched a plot to trounce him thoroughly, which, by the grace of the village goddess, Ma Rajrajeshwari, soon succeeded only too well: the Das houses, though separate, were absolutely cheek-by-jowl, as it happens with the houses of co-tenants, and the enemy camp had got information that Beni had set out to go somewhere and then for some reason hadn't gone but turned back midway; hence this conspiracy of someone posing as Harimati's paramour, these whispered calls, and so on.

Soon after Beni is sentenced to hanging, the break-up begins. The Dases start to move house. All go; there remain only two households—the single Subal, and Gopal Das with his wife and daughters.

Gopal is twice-married. The first wife died in childbirth. The second wife is Kanchan.

Kanchan,[2] indeed…

She is all the beauty, proportion and fullness that man's mind is capable of imagining in a woman's body, her face, her every limb. She indeed seems to be the very image of that vision of the human mind. And just as marvellous are her wits.

After two daughters have been born of Kanchan's womb, Gopal is one day laid by the holy basil.[3] It is a memorable year; cow plague is all the rage in the land.

Gopal has married off one daughter; but he himself is dispatched before he can dispatch the second one. That younger daughter of his, Khushi,[4] is at this time only five years old.

Subal Das comes forward in these difficult days of the widowed Kanchan. He sends word that he wants to marry Khushi. Kanchan has no reason to disagree—save one. In all respects Subal is a likeable match, with capital handsome looks, a farm, and fair means; only he's much older, twenty-three or twenty-four. And Khushi is five.

But Kanchan, thinking it over, at last persuades herself that such a thing, in fact, happens quite often. So-and-so's marriage, so-and-so's son's or brother's or nephew's marriage was just like this—the groom a burly youth, the bride a mere mite.

As soon as Kanchan gives her consent, Subal buys straw and bamboo, engages hut-builders, gets the thatch re-done and the posts replaced, and spruces up her house into tip-top order. And then he goes through the seven circumambulations.[5]

But after the wedding, people laugh themselves to death over Khushi's doings. She addresses Subal by name, calls him *tui*,[6] and goes about from one neighbourhood to another perched on his shoulder.

On market days she says, "Subal, won't tui go to market?"

Subal says, "Yes."

"Bring a paisa's *batasa*[7] for me, I'll eat."

"Okay."

"Tui won't bring. O Ma, look, Subal won't bring batasa."

"When did I say I won't?"

"Then why did tui laugh?"

Some such banter takes place every day. Kanchan listens and laughs. Being of the same neighbourhood, Kanchan and Subal knew each other already, so there isn't much shyness now.

Happily the days go by.

Subal stocks the harvest of his fields and the fruits of his trees in this house. The joys of the little family sparkle around Khushi. Laughter flows over—there isn't a trace of a tear.

But it suddenly makes its appearance one day.

As Subal straightens up, grabbing the basket of rice with both hands and lifting it, meaning to place it on top of the barrel, some bone in his waist snaps with a sharp sound and he starts writhing in pain, just like the severed tail of a gecko. Kanchan screams out, "*Hai hai*!", and cannot make out whether to bathe and fan Subal's head or to apply oil and turps on his waist. Khushi begins to cry, "Ma, Subal is dying!"

Anyway, it's oil massage that is finally decided upon.

Subal's injury is most serious. In the daytime, busy with sundry chores, he doesn't feel the pain so much; but in the evening, having washed his hands and feet, just when he tries to relax, he can neither stand nor sit, and can do nothing but lie down and smoke the hookah, poor thing.

Such is the severity of the affliction when an unthinkable, serious event comes to pass. Subal suddenly sits up and grabs the very hand with which Kanchan is massaging oil on his waist.

But this isn't fortuitous; we know Subal's mind.

Even if the looks of Kanchan's daughter, Khushi, were to replicate in every particular of grace and form the looks of the mother, like flame born of flame, she is due to become housewife a very long time after the marriage. Nobody wants a soulmate these days; the likes of Subal want one even less; there'd be no cause for complaint if she were just able to husk *dhaan*,[8] boil rice and lay it before her husband when he returned from work; but even this competence will take a while to develop in Khushi. Still, Subal has married Khushi only because he thinks that at the right age she will become something of a beauty—this is what people imagine. But Subal's motive was different from the beginning. His target was Kanchan. And other than marrying Khushi there was no way he could have her within his reach all the time.[9] The pain in his waist is also, of course, a sham. To bring Kanchan into close proximity, it was essential, indeed, to make up the excuse of a waist pain.

But when the consequence of this far-reaching scheme of his mind suddenly materialises, assuming an utterly barbarous form, it does, of course, alarm one but, not stopping at that, also fetches the other a blow. Subal is thrown back flat on the mat by a tremendous shove from Kanchan. She comes out trembling. Her eyes stare unblinkingly into the dark emptiness, lightning flashing in them. They don't fill with tears immediately.

We don't know about earlier times, but now the complete futility of her life begins to slowly come back, as if from another world, in incoherent, vague and incomplete forms. Even in the flaming, exuberant passions of youth, she didn't notice how profound, how arid and how thirsty was the emptiness of the nectar cup that had once yearned to be filled to the brim. Today, from where are the anguished sighs of that yawning void rushing in so furiously, trying to tear up her very foundations with blow upon blow!

Kanchan's throat dries up in fear. Her eyes fill with tears, but her whole body burns with anger, too.

Khushi is sleeping; suddenly Kanchan goes and snatches her up to her breast and, hugging her with both arms, keeps shedding tears on her head.

The pot isn't put on the fire that night.

An hour after daybreak.

Khushi comes crying and, hugging Kanchan, says, "Ma, Subal's kicked me." Hearing this, Kanchan is shaken from head to foot by violent rage. This is the first time Subal has tortured his child-wife. In their society, the female body isn't inviolate; beating is a matter of course. But Kanchan goes berserk as she senses with every fibre of her heart the mentality with which Subal has commenced this torture today, even as the darkness suddenly lifts and Subal's deeply buried ulterior motive behind marrying Khushi becomes transparent and clear to her eyes. Kanchan shudders.

When Kanchan rushes out in search of Subal with the girl in her arms, the girl has stopped screaming and, looking with frightened eyes at her mother's face, is just sobbing away. Such horrifying, cataclysmic gloom she has never seen in that face before.

But Subal isn't found; right after planting the kick he has gone out. Kanchan comes back and tells her daughter, "Hold on, let him come, then I'll see." But it doesn't relieve the girl's misery.

When Subal returns, Kanchan is picking grit from lentils spread on a tray. Subal's heart is in a flutter. That sound isn't heard; only the sound of his footsteps keeps approaching. Kanchan cannot turn her eyes that way, but her heart, opening a thousand eyes as it were, turns around to watch his sweat-bathed exhaustion and parching thirst.

Continuing to pick grit from the lentils, Kanchan says in a normal enough tone, "There's your water and *gur*[10] covered under the stool. Don't take it yet; let the sweat die out first."

Until now Subal was carrying about in his breast a heavy lump of an intolerable apprehension, so that there was no limit to his unease. As he had no inkling as to which weapon—from a bullock-driving goad to the club of a *dhenki*[11]—would be deemed potent enough to accompany her verbal venom, his mental agony didn't abate one bit, but only multiplied.

The sweat on his body will die out by and by. For the moment, at Kanchan's normal words, the living lump of fear and anxiety dies out to revive him. Fanning himself with his towel, Subal is entering his room when Khushi rushes in from somewhere crying, "Ma, there, Subal's come."

Hearing this, Subal turns his face with a smirk and slips into the room, but Kanchan's lowered gaze hardens and many harsh words line up at the tip of her tongue.

At one go he drinks off a jug of water in noisy gulps, and then, just as he lets out a loud *Ah* of satisfaction, Kanchan says from the veranda, "Why did you kick Khushi?"

Subal has his answer ready. He says, "I don't like the whining day and night."

Although Khushi is very small, and his wife by marriage, Subal is nervous inside because there is no saying whether an explanation based simply on his dislike will work or not. But it does seem to work. On Kanchan's part there is no objection or protest to his answer.

Greatly amused and chuckling, Subal quietly gets up and peeps at Kanchan through the door, and stops dead. He sees there is a reason why Kanchan hasn't spoken: her body is being convulsed with a fit of silent crying.

With a face as if smeared with a mass of grime, Subal slinks away like a thief. Last evening's offence, which till then didn't seem so grave to his boorish mind, now suddenly becomes a matter of such shame at the sight of Kanchan crying that it seems no longer possible even to come out of the room and face her.

Khushi comes and says, "Subal, go for your bath—Ma said."

Subal is lying on his back; he doesn't stir at the command sent via Khushi.

A little later Khushi comes again, this time with a cup of oil, and says, "Subal, go for your bath, quick. Ma said if tui are so scared, don't do it again."

A hot flush runs through Subal's heart. Immediately, he shakes himself and hurriedly sits up, looking wide-eyed at Khushi.

Even though it is totally impossible, he longs so much to go and hear for once with his own ears in what tone Kanchan has spoken these words, and see with his own eyes the expression on her face at the time. It seems there is a ring of forgiveness in these words. Khushi has given just a bald message, but how was the face then—stern or tender or what?

Seeing the delay, Kanchan herself now comes up. Standing outside the door, she says, "Just tell me whether you're going to eat or not, I'll be relieved. I have enough work besides serving your meal." But with unbearable self-reproach Kanchan keeps feeling she hasn't been able to remain as stern as she ought to have. She isn't doing her duty towards the daughter of her womb. How very helpless and immature the child! The seed of desire, other than that for play, has not yet sprouted in her. It is Kanchan's responsibility to properly punish the man who is constantly looking to spoil the purity of that future desire with the contagion of his filthy heart. Utterly loathsome is the man who so freely raises his hand to defile today what is still so far away.[12]

After his bath, Subal returns to find his rice has been left covered, though it wouldn't be so every day. Khushi is on guard against cats.

While taking his bath in the warm water of the dried-up riverbed, Subal further lightened his heart by puffing it up with his high spirits; he even forgot for a while to take a second dip after the first. But he is quite crestfallen at not finding, in actual fact, any sign of the welcome he expected.

"Where's your Ma, huh?" he asks.

"Don't know," says Khushi. "Make your *paan*[13] yourself." But there's no longer any relish for rice or any desire for paan left in Subal.

Kanchan returns to find that Subal hasn't eaten even a fourth of the rice. But by then her exhausted mind is, as it were, lying limply prostrate, its eyes shut. Her heart, out of just numb lethargy, refuses to entertain any regret even at the fact that somebody has got up without eating his meal.

The door of Subal's room has been put to. Opening it slightly, Kanchan finds Subal and Khushi sleeping side by side—Subal's face dejected, Khushi's smiling. The sight is at once as pathetic as it is comical.

When Kanchan comes away, putting the door to again, her outer as well as her inner world, her blood as well as her heart, has been convulsed into a great awakening, shattering the boundless torpor of exhaustion. Suddenly her eyes open to the extreme cruelty of the whole affair. Husband and wife sleeping in the same bed. It seems as if one of them has just fallen asleep in utter weariness after rebelling against a heartless, spiritless world, with full-blown manhood and virility manifest all over his body. Beside him lies a mere child. Kanchan's feet refuse to move forward. Turning back, she pushes open the door of Subal's bedroom and gingerly picks up the girl. But the moment she steps out with the girl in her arms, she loses all sense of the state of her own mind. In the midday sun, as if chased by a ghost behind, she rushes on towards nowhere like a leaf blown by a storm wind. Where she'll stop remains entirely outside her thoughts.

Subal wakes up to find the house deserted. Cows, using the opportunity, have entered the house and all but finished off the dhaan laid out in the sun. He bawls out a few times, "Khushi?"

But Khushi is then in her mother's arms, on the veranda of an old neighbour.

Kanchan, of course, can't be called; she'll have to be sought out quietly. Before marriage, he used to call Kanchan by name. Desire was then awake in his heart, but it hadn't got so passionately entwined with the name. Now his very faculty of speech throbs to call her over by name. But that path is closed.[14] Now he calls Khushi, but whatever he says is meant for Kanchan. It serves in a way.

After calling for Khushi and getting no response, Subal looks about here and there, in this room and that. Khushi and her mother are nowhere.

He will speak his mind clearly enough on whether one should go out of the house leaving the dhaan unguarded in the sun, but he won't betray even the slightest anger. Having made this resolution, Subal washes his hands and face, makes up a paan, puts it in his mouth and has just lit his hubble-bubble when Khushi's voice is heard outside, "Ma, see if my lips are red with paan juice?"

Kanchan is coming. At the mere sound of it, Subal's resolution gives way to tremendous resentment over the dhaan. Dhaan of such hard labour.

But Khushi comes in alone.

Subal says, "Where's your Ma?"

"Ma's standing there. Ma's asked you to go to your own house; else she won't come."

"Indeed?" Subal roars out and keeps shouting, "Would anyone but a thankless female do such a thing? Okay, I'm going, right now. No more in your house, no more with you. What you live on, I'll see. I'll sit and see who stuffs your pot-belly with the harvest of his field and vegetables of his garden. Treachery with me!" But his anger dies out as he speaks, and tears well up from somewhere to flood his eyes.

Khushi says, "Go right now. Ma..." She has scarcely turned to the hurried footsteps behind her when, with a smart slap on her back, Kanchan lifts her up in the air and goes away just as hurriedly.

Kanchan hasn't seen with her own eyes the pain in Subal's face, but has heard his voice and how that voice abruptly stopped, choked with tears. Suddenly something happens inside her breast, as if someone was wringing it turn upon turn. But while instructing Khushi to say those words she didn't even remotely imagine that her own words would turn so unbearably harsh as they entered her ears from someone else's mouth. Then, despite all her anger, she inwardly smiled a little: Can he do it? No; whatever else he may do he won't be able to go out of her sight.

But before the test of whether he can do it is over, Kanchan has to change her tune.

Khushi comes to say, "Ma's asked you not to go."

Subal doesn't utter a word, doesn't lift a hand to wipe his eyes, doesn't even raise his eyes to look. Insult and ingratitude have hit him hard. But he cannot remain silent for long either. He comes out with Khushi and says, "I'm not serving anyone's whims that whenever I am ordered to get out, I'll get out, and if the next moment I am ordered to stay back, I'll stay back. Why, what's my obligation?"

Having posed the question, Subal starts puffing frenziedly at his hubble-bubble. After a little delay comes the answer to his question.

Still remaining out of sight, Kanchan says, "You have no obligation; all obligations are mine, I know it. But you should have gone before I asked. You haven't got the sense of a human being—if you had, you'd have done so."

Subal says, "Nobody can beat you in quarrel, certainly not me, that's a known fact. But what is my offence?"

This question from Subal is as daring as it is brazen. Subal's inner world is thrown wide open to Kanchan's eyes. She clearly sees that a long-nursed desire, fed full on crookedness and deceit and creeping up slowly like a snail, has, all of a sudden, reared up.

The hairs stand on end on Kanchan's body.

Her anger at the shameless, easy insolence of the depraved man knows no bounds. No words come to her lips; who knows what the tone would have been if they did. Trembling, she only moves up two steps and, raising a finger, points at Subal's abandoned house. Then, entering her room with quick steps, she slumps to the floor and keeps saying, "God, save me, save me."

Khushi comes and informs her, "Ma, Subal's gone away."

She hoped her mother would jump at the good news but she is disappointed.

Khushi calls again, "Ma, get up, do, Subal's gone."

"Gone?" Saying this, Kanchan raises her eyes and immediately turns them away.

Khushi is a small girl. It isn't possible for her to be inquisitive or suspicious about the bloodshot eyes; but with unbounded inner agony, Kanchan feels there is no greater deception or sin on earth than showing these eyes to a daughter.

All day long there are no sounds of Subal.

After dusk one can hear slight movements and one sees smoke coming out through the innumerable openings of Subal's hut. Kanchan cannot bear to look at that smoke.[15]

Through the unremitting activity of daytime, her mind remains constantly charged with the sense of a single direction like a compass needle. A faint sound, no matter where…immediately Kanchan's ears, mind, nerves, consciousness wake up with wide-open eyes in every hair of her body. The more the day wears on, the keener becomes her mind. Her millstones grate. Her broom swishes. Her utensils clatter. But beyond all these sounds, a most minute sound, a sign of homecoming, a tired little humming keep ceaselessly arising on the far horizon of her fancies. Suddenly she stops: the sound is there, it seems! The next moment there's no end to her disappointment and distress: maybe she's missed the first sound she so much hoped for. Leaving her work, she keeps her ears pricked up for a long time.

Suddenly one day neither any sound comes nor any smoke rises at the usual hour.

After fidgeting about from one room to another for a while, Kanchan calls Khushi and says, "Can't hear any sound in that house. Go see if Subal's come." Khushi runs off, and presently runs back to report, "Subal's not come, Ma."

"Let's go and look," so saying Kanchan herself goes to Subal's house with Khushi.

The moment she unfastens the kitchen door, she can't hold back her tears at the sight that suddenly opens before her eyes. On a banana leaf a heap of bare uneaten rice has dried stiff, and rats have scattered rice all over the room.

It is last evening's meal. A whole day has passed since.

Looking at the heap of rice, Kanchan's eyes glaze over. After staring at it for some time, she says, "Bring a little cow-dung,[16] Khushi, let's clean up the leavings."

But Subal's missus has her objections to it. She says, "But it is Subal's house, Ma."

"Let it be, bring it." So saying Kanchan starts wiping up the leavings, but the work isn't finished. Khushi has gone down to the courtyard in search of cow-dung; from there she cries out, "Ma, Subal's come." And she begins to giggle.

The matter isn't at all clear to Khushi. But some hide-and-seek has been going on and Subal's turning up just at that moment has put her mother in a spot—this much is apparent even to Khushi's immature understanding.

Subal goes up straight into the room. Kanchan has then stood up. The two stand face to face—two pairs of eyes meet. Subal's face, filling up with an amused smile, suddenly turns grave; and all the sensations of Kanchan's body and mind keep spinning around a single point like an eddy of water in a swift current. Just as countless small and big things drawn with inexorable speed from afar rush into the bowels of whirling water to disappear in the blink of an eye, so a titanic force begins its invincible action all over Kanchan's consciousness. In an instant her world, her past, present and future are totally obliterated, leaving only a luminous point imprinted on her vision.

Khushi cries out from the courtyard, "Ma, look who's come!"

Subal moves aside. At once, pulling herself together, Kanchan comes out; but the traces of the smothering vortex which has just cast up and released her cannot be effaced so easily.

The visitor woman keeps a sharp eye on Kanchan's face but points her question at Khushi, "Who else in the room, eh? Durga, Durga.[17] Will come some other day, Kanchan. Landed up at a very odd time today. You'll perhaps go for a wash now?" She curls her lips in a chuckle and conspicuously covers it with the end of her sari.

Kanchan thinks, I've deserved this. Now the penance begins. She says, "No, Aunt, let's go to my house. I came to clean up Subal's leavings."

Aunt said, "Oh sure, why else would you come at this hour? I'll come tomorrow. Had no great business." While saying this, Kanchan's aunt shoots an oblique glance at Kanchan's grubby hands and walks out in a one-two, one-two step.

Kanchan stands rooted in the middle of the courtyard, motionless and pale, as though there's no life in her body.

Khushi starts pushing her with both hands, "Ma, let's go, I'm scared."

Kanchan once looks back at the house from which she has just come out with the burden of scandal on her head. She can't make out a thing in the dark.

Kanchan dreads to look at Khushi.

She's all right at night. The curtain of darkness, secluding her completely, draws, as it were, a long, firm parting line around the place of her contact with the earth, and she finds relief in hiding.

But the clear view of her body in the clear light of day gives an eerie feeling to her soul. Her hand recoils, as if pushed, as it rises to touch Khushi; she feels some unknown poison will rain down through her touch on her daughter's life, causing her no end of harm. It seems Khushi is a sacrificial kid and Karali,[18] burning with thirst, tongue perpetually lolling, is eyeing her budding life. Kanchan closes her eyes with a sudden shiver and, with eyes closed, she looks at herself. She sees a boundless uncharted wasteland in which there is nowhere a sound or mist or coolness or movement; glaring sunlight has created a mirage of a transparent lake in the middle. Hairs stand on end all over her shivering body. Opening her eyes, she says, "Come, Khushi, let's go for a walk." So saying, with Khushi in front, she roams the paths of the village like a lost traveller.

By now Subal has gained a rough knowledge of Kanchan's mind. Even a barbarian couldn't but understand, at least partly, such an intense exposure of the mind. But how keen it is and how amenable, where lies its impediment, where the aversion and where the hazard—it isn't possible for the blind Subal to even remotely approach such fine discriminations and nuances.

This doesn't prevent him one bit from cheering up, but the fear isn't entirely gone either. His hope, for the time when the favourable call would unmistakably come dispelling all fears and doubts, becomes so acute that he is thrown into a state of extreme restlessness.

Subal has given up going to work.

Khushi comes now and then to pick up and take home a coconut shell or a fruit lying under the tree. Whenever Subal sees her coming, he asks, "Has your Ma called me?"

"No," says Khushi.

"Then why are you here?" With a spring Subal lands on the courtyard from the veranda.

Khushi runs away.

Kanchan comes and says, "Take care: lay your hands on Khushi and you've had it."

In time Subal grows thievish—snooping around, peeping and looking for the propitious moment.

Kanchan hasn't been keeping well. Her eyes have sunk in, her complexion has dulled; a wasting dryness is engulfing her body. She often has sudden fits of dizziness and black-outs.

With such immense exhaustion and weakness in every part of her body, she's lying down. The clay lamp in the room is burning feebly. Khushi has fallen asleep. Trembling, Subal climbs on to

Kanchan's veranda. Silently positioning his eyes at the door, he sees Kanchan lying with her eyes shut, clothes not in place.

Standing stiff for a moment before the closed door, Subal pushes it ajar. Opening her eyes at the sound and seeing Subal right in front of the door, Kanchan hastily draws her clothes over her body and sits up. And the next moment the voice that erupts from her throat, breaking through all her torpor, is such as Subal has never heard issuing from a human mouth. Kanchan screams—"Go, go, go away from me! Go at once! Go I say, go, go—."

At her voice and at what little can be seen of Kanchan's face in the dim light of the clay lamp, Subal gives a start and is totally petrified. There seems nothing but fierce bloodlust in her look.

Kanchan's weak brain cannot take so much excitement. The scream, rising to the highest pitch of her voice, abruptly stops and she faints and collapses on the spot.

But Subal's animality by then has reached the peak of frenzy.

The two no longer speak. Immense restless disquiet has turned into lifeless stone like a palace under curse.

Bamandas Adhikari's nickname is Juju.[19] The word is small in size but profound in meaning. Under Bamandas' power a tiger and a cow may not drink at the same water-hole, but there is surely no way a transgression can occur within the four boundaries of the village.

It is Bamandas who owns the land under the homes of Subal and Kanchan. At first, he didn't hear anything about the latest moral affliction of the village. Aunt hadn't talked even after witnessing the incident of that day with her own eyes. She knew there's God, and some day or other He'd bring forth the fruit of sin in the sinner's body itself.

Aunt's hope has been brought to fruition. And it is Aunt's eyes which detect this.

Passing from ear to ear, word one day gets into Bamandas' ears as well, and the lord of the land springs off the land and becomes as angry as the inflamed Fire-God. Had there been matted hair on his head,[20] it would surely have shot up to hit the heavens. "Round 'em up!" he roars out his order and gets, first the 'sinner woman', and then Subal, arrested and brought in.

Aunt is also there. As soon as she sees Kanchan, she hides her face in modesty, slips out to take cover and crouches down to lie in wait.

Bamandas speaks, and the words, as it were, keep beating their heads on the true-souled great man's holy feet: "Can a man go near a woman without her indulgence? Why don't you speak, filthy hag?"

Divine energy in the form of The Word keeps pouring out of his mouth in such free flow that people in the house—even if they don't stop their ears with a shudder—are left dumbstruck.

And then, grabbing Kanchan by the hair and flinging her on the ground, he gives her such a beating with his wooden sandal that even a ghost that no thrashing can exorcise would have taken to its heels just at the sight of it.

Tiring, Bamandas sits down for a while; Subal will be dealt with later.

Kanchan's body splits open and blood pours out.

Facing her bloody body lying in the dust sit a trembling Bamandas on one side and a speechless Subal on the other. Looking dazedly at the stream of blood, Subal suddenly cries out, "Aaah! Haaa!" and, falling across Bamandas feet, says, "It is all my fault, beat me too!"

That it is all Subal's fault is not, of course, believed by Bamandas. Kicking Subal aside, he says, "Great attachment, I say! My name is Bamandas Adhikari. I understand everything, know everything. The golden Lanka was ravaged for her; the

Kuru family, too, was destroyed for her.[21] Don't any of you come to teach me anything. If the woman doesn't bewitch, does a man become sheep just like that? Bastard, you, too, have lost your wits?"

Bamandas' desire for beating has been spent on Kanchan. Having spelt out the cause of the ravage of the golden Lanka and of the destruction of the Kuru family, and having reprimanded Subal for his brainlessness, he calls out, "Hey, who is there?"

Defaulting debtor Bhim Das is there in attendance. Spotting him, Bamandas orders, "Call up Shasthi, Phatik, Manik, Nibaran, all of them. And catch hold of whoever else you meet on the way."

Interest liabilities are a great obligation. Even before the words can properly end on Bamandas' lips, Bhim Das shoots out like an arrow.

Catching hold of Shasthi, Phatik, Manik, Nibaran and whoever else he meets on the way, Bhim Das fills Bamandas' house with people in no time. Bamandas says, "Come along." With that, he himself goes ahead, axe in hand, and under his leadership, Shasthi, Phatik, Manik, Nibaran, all of them together raze the huts and kitchens of Kanchan and Subal to the ground in two minutes. The children, the old, the women of the village stand and witness this retribution of sin.

Coming back, Bamandas addresses Shasthi, Phatik, Manik, Nibaran and the rest of the crowd and says, "Each of you go give a kick on this hussy's back."

But nobody carries out his order; perhaps no one can lift their feet looking at the blood-smeared cloth on her back.

Only Aunt says from a distance, "O Ma, what again!"

Then Bamandas himself gives a kick on Kanchan's back and a punch on Subal's neck and says, "My job is done only after I've packed them off across the boundary of the village. Go, get up." So saying, he keeps his finger raised and pointing towards the western boundary of the village.

Khushi, lying on her back in her mother's lap, is then heard saying, "Ma, get up, let's go home."

Notes

1. The material used for it would typically be bamboo.

2. It means 'gold', a common endearment as well as a metaphor for beauty.

3. Dying people are so laid for the salvation of their souls.

4. Meaning 'joy'.

5. A rite solemnising a marriage. The groom and bride walk together seven times around the sacred fire.

6. A variant of 'you', signifying an intimacy of equals or disparagement, depending upon the context. And therefore, it was never used to address the husband.

7. Sugar drop, a cheap sweet.

8. Unhusked rice.

9. Despite vigorous efforts at reform, the remarriage of a widow was practically impossible in orthodox Hindu society, and is not always easy even now.

10. Jaggery.

11. The simple Indian husking machine, consisting of a wooden see-saw, fitted at one end with a heavy club for pounding the rice, and worked at the other end by women with their feet.

12. The author's precise meaning here is somewhat obscure.

13. See note 10, 'Son and Son's Wife'.

14. Because now she is his mother-in-law, and no senior may be addressed by name.

15. Because a man is trying, clumsily, to do a woman's job of lighting the fire and cooking.

16. The leavings of a meal are exceedingly unclean; cow-dung is a purifier.

17. The supreme mother goddess whose name is frequently invoked to ward off a calamity or evil.

18. 'The Fearsome She', another name of Kali, the goddess of massacre, who, with lolling tongue, licks her victims' blood. In the past, humans were sometimes sacrificed to her; young goats still routinely are. More in note 2, 'Mrs Havoc'.

19. Meaning 'bogey'.

20. As god-men have.

21. Allusions to the epics *Ramayana* and *Mahabharata* in which two women are at the centre of two wars.

A Bond Defiled*

[1] After a long one-and-a-half years, Satkari will return home tomorrow morning.

To explain where he's been all these days, one has to narrate the incident of Madhudanga.[2]

In which era, in whose times, during which king's reign the visitation of Madhu took place—no one from these parts has so much as felt the need for doing any research on this until now. Whether Madhu was a Hindu or a Muslim, an *Ugrakshatriya* or a *Sadgop*,[3] no one knows even that. They only know that long ago a formidable bandit named Madhu lived in this place. The name of the place had earlier been Pitambarpur. Later, the name after Madhu gained currency, and everyone now calls it Madhudanga.

Somewhere in this treeless, grassless, intractable heath extending to the horizon there was, it is said, Madhu's fort under the ground. No government spy could ever seek out the fort or the master of the fort, Madhu.

*Published in Bengali posthumously in 1959 as *Kalankita Samparka.* Originally it had been published under a different title, *Ahuti*, c1930.

Madhu is gone, but Madhudanga remains. And at this small, wayside village of Madhudanga, a fair is held on the *Jhulan*[4] day. But the fair of Madhudanga is a fair in name only. It is nothing much, just ten or twelve stalls. People bring in—some on their heads or backs, some on ox-carts—cooking utensils like tubs and pans, various kinds of toys, mirror-fronted tin boxes, wooden combs and lockets, ribbons and waist cords, needles and thread, chips and mushy peas, betel leaves and cigarettes, sweets of diverse shape, taste, colour and smell, and whatever else might tempt and be purchased by boys and girls and householders. And they just rig up a piece of sack cloth and sit down.

There is, however, more grandeur inside: the capacious, towering temple with the images of Radha and Krishna; right in front of it the *kirtan*[5]-pavilion; on one side of it the courtyard; and south of the courtyard the guesthouse—a place for *Vaishnav*[6] mendicants to rest and eat.

As soon as dusk fell, huge lamps were lit and the kirtan began. Innumerable people had sat down to partake in the bliss and felicity of the kirtan: a mother had turned up with a month-and-a-half-old baby and, not to speak of the able-bodied, even a blind old man of more than a hundred years had been brought and seated bang in the front by the members of his family.

Lots of people were at the kirtan, but not everybody. Outside, here and there under the trees, sat the Vaishnav patriarchs with their consorts—having no work to do, they were busy chatting. Elsewhere, some others had laid bricks to knock up a fire and were boiling rice in a wok—unlike the patriarchs and their consorts, they hadn't been invited to receive Krishna's *prasad*.[7] The place had become very filthy with smoke and dust. The others who were outside looked as if they were all fagged out: those who walked, walked with dangling limbs; those who sat, sat with drooping head; those who lay, lay with backs bent, head to knees; a beggar woman sat impassively looking at her son who was picking up dust and putting it into his mouth.

The shops were open, however. A widowed girl of twenty-two or twenty-three sat in front of a trinket stall, choosing waist cords for someone. Having chosen a pair, she stood up to find a strange man standing close by. The girl moved away.

That very man, a stranger to the girl, was Satkari. With two bosom buddies he had come to the Madhudanga fair to have fun. What kind of fun he had had till then and what kind of fun he would have had all night nobody knows, not even he himself. But that the climax to the fun was rudely thwarted is known to everyone. He and his cronies had to go to Giridharpur police station just when they were trying to achieve the climax. The fun wasn't consummated; for a grievous crime Satkari was given a jail sentence by the court.

After serving the sentence—that is, after all relish for fun has been wrung out—Satu will come home tomorrow. In the house some know, and some don't, what day of the month it is today. Yet, someone among these many, it seems, has been quietly keeping track and has suddenly put it about that Satu will come home tomorrow. Tomorrow is the 7th.

Of four brothers, Satkari is the second. His two younger brothers live away from home. Still, the house is crowded, and Satkari's wife, too, is in the crowd.

Satkari's wife, Makhanbala, had also been counting the days, but in a different way. Nervously, with a trembling heart, she had been counting the days that remained before she would see her husband again. One day, dazed by the counting, she forgot to count. The initial context she remembered, and the day at the end of her counting loomed up like a spectre, and she was racked by the shivers it sent through her heart. But the countless days in between passed by insensibly one after the other. She didn't want to think any more. Shutting her mind's eye and blinding herself, she desperately buried in an infinite darkness the day that lay at the end of these numberless days. Suddenly from that darkness, that terrible day has reared its head. Makhan gives a start. A short night in between. Tomorrow the sun will rise again. Then her husband will come.

Makhan's parched, dead-alive heart is in her mouth. Life, and the days between a sunrise and a sunset, never seemed so brief to her. It was just morning on the day Satkari went, and it is evening now. Makhan feels she has let out just one sigh in between. But the sigh hasn't been let out fully; her breast is unbearably heavy with the burden of the breath. Meanwhile one-and-a-half years have gone by!

There are more people in the house, all Satu's own: someone, his brother; another, his sister-in-law; this, his mother; that, something else. Yet, in spite of there being so many near relations, Makhan feels that her involvement with the whole affair is greater than anybody else's—she is the one most entangled in it. She is his wife. Nobody perhaps ever sat down to figure out consciously which area of her husband's life she, coming in from outside, had occupied. Still, people seemed to expect an absoluteness of her dominion in a certain realm—that in that realm she would be all-possessing, all-consuming, ever-vigilant. It seemed as simple and unqualified a fact as human consciousness itself that she would exact her due to the fullest by grabbing, wrenching and wresting it with ten hands like the all-powerful ten-armed goddess[8] rather than renouncing even an iota of her claim and putting up with any infringement of her claims.

But she hasn't been able to demonstrate that power and for this disgraceful inability has had to hang her head before everyone in the world. Many a time after her marriage, her mother-in-law hinted and suggested to her that it was she who must provide the son's life with its moorings and order, that she must be the custodian of the grace, beauty and dignity of good form. Everyone was of this opinion; those outside the family, too, had the same wish, the same view. Superseding the mother, superseding an elder brother and two younger brothers, she had become all. Nobody had any reservations, hesitation or doubt about giving up this topmost and foremost place unconditionally to a single person and freeing themselves of all concerns. Her mother-in-law was in fact relieved—as if her existence alone was an inviolable, invincible decree that would be impossible to transgress.

But she's defeated today, her sceptre biting the dust. Today she's so insignificant, unimportant and useless that it's all the same whether she exists or not. What the world is saying or thinking, she doesn't know; but she herself isn't able to stand apart autonomously, detaching herself from her husband's life! Her world is extremely small. Only with her husband as her stalk did she connect with the living world that lay outside his being; only with her husband as her stalk did she open out to the surrounding atmosphere. This was her very identity.

And this identity had been continuing.

Then suddenly one day it happened. The earth went off its orbit to turn over upside down. She had been happy and normal precisely because all things were arrayed in their place. But then, in a blink of the eye, they were thrown into a monstrous confusion and her world turned into a desolate cremation ground for the dead.

Her husband went to jail.

Her grove, resonant with the humming music of bees, wilted under the terrible blow; her sky, replete with garlands of light, banks of cloud and tremors of wind, disappeared in darkness; the unique nest woven with flowers of thought and thirst of the heart vanished without a trace; the daily celebrations in her temple stopped; the sweet sap at the heart of flowers turned bitter; and the path by which light and music reached her sight and hearing and heaven's elixir rained on her was shut out in an instant. She no longer had any connection with the world.

But nobody came forward offering their breast to share her misery. She felt as if an outcry of censure, rising from the centre of their home, had spread out to the farthest reaches of human habitation, to every palace and hut, over all land and sea, up to the very last limiting line where the earth and the sky truly met; and the world of the living, stopping its ears, sat shuddering.

This unbearable shame remains, like a massive monolith, like a dark cloud, permanently occupying her breast alone. Nobody has come up to share the burden saying, "I'm with you."

Her husband's crime is grievous—such as one cannot even bear to think of. No human being could ever condone it. No woman, whether mother of a child or mistress of a family or wife of a man, could excuse it. No one that bears God's name in his heart and the awareness of not having been born a beast could pardon it.

Committing such an unthinkable crime, her husband went to jail. Tomorrow he will be released and will come back. Tomorrow is the 7th.

All the others in the house are in suspense, even the servant. They grew tired of living in dejection and seem to have buried their shame in that tiredness. They don't remember why their dear one hasn't been at home so long.

But it would be better if he had never been there at all.

It is the dead of night. Makhan comes and stands outside. Lifting her eyes up to the sky, she once calls upon God. Every speck of light everywhere in the vast sky has disappeared without a trace behind thick layers of cloud. The world is sunk under a fathomless ocean of darkness; it has stopped breathing.

Makhan feels frightened.

Who are these that have descended into this abyss of darkness and are busy churning? They are looking for their lost treasures.[9] Their hands are soundless, feet are soundless, lips are soundless—only their eyes are flashing on and off. With the pitiless, relentless thrashing of their churning-rod, waves are rushing out from the centre of the vortex, spewing smoke and foamy venom. Holding this blazing venom in a pot, someone is approaching. The dark figure is distinct even in the darkness: silent, firm, unhurried. She must drink the venom, there is no escape. From a measureless distance, pushing through layer after layer of the shroud of darkness, the figure is approaching—there is no pause in its motion—as if it must keep coming eternally, there being no end to its path. When will it arrive right in front of her and put the pot of venom in her hands!

Her elder sister-in-law, Golap, gets up first. Coming down onto the courtyard, she lets out a cry. Awakened by the cry, everyone rushes out and finds Makhan lying senseless in the courtyard.

The mother-in-law runs out and sits down, taking the daughter-in-law's head in her lap. Won't her son come today, very soon! Today is the 7th.

Golap hauls up three buckets of water in two minutes.

Nitu puts his hand on Makhan's face and keeps calling, "Auntie? Auntie?"

Satkari's elder brother, Satish, pops his face out from behind the door, and withdraws immediately.

Pushing Nitu aside, Golap begins to pour water on Makhan's head. Biraj begins to fan. After a short while Makhan opens her eyes and sits up; she can't make out whether the scene that is coming to her mind really happened, or if she saw it in a dream.

Biraj asks, "How do you feel, daughter?"

Makhan's mind is in a fog. She takes time to form the words for an answer. Biraj asks the same question again; but before Makhan can say anything, Satish comes down.

Biraj says, "Where are you going?"

"To bring Satu, Ma…"

"Go."

Satish asks, "How did Sister come to faint in the yard?"

"That's what I'm asking her. Don't worry, she's okay,"—that is, concern for Sister needn't delay his going to bring Satkari.

"I'm going," Satish says, and goes out.

No one knows if Satu will need to be dragged in, but he might well feel uncomfortable to enter the house all by himself, like someone uninvited. So Biraj and her eldest son Satish, after consultations, are making a simple, little gesture to forestall this. Satish goes ahead to bring him.

Biraj and the elder daughter-in-law then turn on Makhan.

"Felt sick?"

Makhan has been sitting like one dead. She says, "No."

"Then? Had a fright?"

"No."

"Then?"

Makhan says, "Couldn't sleep at night, so came and stood outside. Then fainted; when and how, I don't know." With this Makhan gets up.

Nitu starts jumping in joy, holding Makhan's sari.

Very late in the day Satish returns, but alone.

Biraj, relieved that her younger daughter-in-law is moving about normally, has been standing at the door, awaiting her son's homecoming. Seeing Satish return alone, she shrieks out, "Where's Satu?"

Slowly Satish comes and stands beside her and says, "Hasn't come."

"Hasn't come? Where's he gone?"

All these days, the prospect of meeting him and getting him back wasn't imminent, and so the inevitable delay was endurable. But today, drawing nearer every moment, where has he suddenly disappeared instead of materialising right in front of her? Biraj's heart feels like bursting.

Satish says, "Telling you, let's go inside."

As soon as they go in, Biraj asks again, "Why couldn't you bring him? Where's he gone?"

"Don't know where he's gone! Coming out of the jail, he said, 'Wait a bit, I'm coming,' and went away, who knows on what business. My plight, standing and standing..."

What plight befell him as he stood there waiting for Satu, he doesn't elaborate. Perhaps disconcerted by the tears in his mother's eyes, he slinks away.

Biraj says, "Maybe he came right back and, not finding you, went off somewhere else."

Biraj's conjecture is not true, of course, but no reply comes from Satish.

The tears that then appear in her eyes don't stop, nor does she make any attempt to stop them. With the tears flowing, the sighs keep blowing, too.

But what becomes more unbearable to Makhan than all her misery and desperation is this painful thought:[10] what kind of son is this who has plunged them all in mire, and then parades them in full view of the world! These tears are an insult to humanity of all times and all places, the blackest blot on maternal affection. Indecent are these tears.

At one point, as Biraj is wiping her eyes, Makhan says, "You're waiting for him in vain, Ma. He can't come in broad daylight in front of people. He'll come after dark."

Biraj hears, and seethes in her guts. She has been watching her daughter-in-law's ways. At these words, she fixes her with fiercer eyes and says, "Daughter, I don't like your sulks and tantrums. Your mouth's dripping poison. Don't be so foul-mouthed. You can't go to my son with such a foul mouth, I tell you. Know your place. We're your elders. In our presence..." But when she sees Makhan abruptly turn away she steers her speech onto a different tack and delivers her final words, very brief and forceful: "Go, but take care."

The moment things quieten a bit, Satish cranes his neck and asks, "What is it, Ma?"

"I'll come and tell you", so saying Biraj sits down to pour into her elder son's ears her hurt and grievance over her younger daughter-in-law's behaviour, but receives neither hurt nor comfort. Satish, embarrassed at this muckraking, says, "Tell your elder daughter-in-law,[11] she'll talk it over with her." So saying, he lowers his face.

Unable to withstand the silent tears of his mother and the pestering of all the others, Satish goes out to look for his brother once again. But the missing man isn't found at any of the prescribed or proscribed, decent or indecent, places. There was not even a clue as to where he could be found. At these tidings,

Biraj takes to her bed, lies there for a while, and then keeps going in and out of her room, again and again. Makhan's manner adds anger to her anxiety, yet her mouth remains wordless and rice doesn't pass through it today.

But Makhan's words do come true.

After dark, sitting near his grandma's lap at the threshold of the main gate, Nitu asks, "When will Uncle come, Grandma? Where's he gone?"

Biraj, dozing as if in a stupor, says, "Don't know."

"Where was he all these days?"

Biraj keeps her face turned aside and doesn't speak.

Nitu goes on: "Uncle hasn't come home for many days, isn't it, Grandma? Why? Where was he all these days? What'll he bring for me?"

Grandma doesn't show any interest in satisfying her dearest little grandson's curiosity. The entreaty and eagerness expressed in hundreds of such questions of the boy that would always stir up the deepest joy in her heart today only weigh down her eyelids insensibly for a moment, and yet she isn't struck by the incongruity of it all. But after he falls silent, the whole house is stilled and Biraj remains distracted.

Biraj was distracted. Suddenly, with a start, she sees a man standing before her, wrapped from head to foot in a sheet of cloth. She doesn't take an instant to recognise him. Crying, "Satu!" she springs up like a real living being. Throwing off the covers from his head and body, Satu bows to his mother's feet, and the next moment the hullabaloo breaks out. Nitu starts loudly broadcasting the news: "Baba, Uncle's come. Ma, Uncle's come. Auntie, Uncle's come," and he starts dancing, holding his uncle's hands and lifting up his face towards his uncle's.

Saying "Come", Biraj strides ahead. Following her, Satu goes inside the house and finds everyone, except his wife, eagerly standing together. He bows to his elder brother's as well as his sister-in-law's feet. When he went, he hadn't seen his brother's youngest son; touching the baby's cheek with two fingers of his right hand he asks, "Now, when did this one turn up?"

His elder brother hasn't much to say. Even in this little time, the bemused question: "Where did you disappear leaving me standing there?" has risen several times in his mind. But, realising the reason for his disappearance, he quietly slips away—in embarrassment, perhaps. He can't mouth any greetings at all, even to please his mother.

Only sister-in-law Golap asks, "Are you well?"

Satu says, "By your blessing," and smiles. The smile suddenly seeming distasteful, Golap's heart becomes sadder. She has work in the kitchen; she goes in there after the indifferent welcome.

Biraj inspects her son. Having neither embarrassment nor work in the kitchen, she runs her hands over his body and says, "You've grown so thin. No disease inside, have you?"

Satu once glances over his body, smiles, and says, "No, but they've tortured me real bad, Ma!"

Tears well up in the mother's eyes and she says, "Have you eaten anything the whole day today?"

What Satu has eaten[12] at their haunt today are not allowed in the house, let alone cooked. He, however, lies: "Nothing at all, Ma."

"Nothing? Oh-ho-ho-ho…," wails Biraj, and then she bawls out, "Makhan, finished cooking?" And without waiting a moment for the answer, she herself goes up and stands at the kitchen door to supervise the cooking. And before she finds out whether the cooking is finished or not, she finds her younger daughter-in-law sitting hunched in a corner, leaning her body against the wall like one racked and enfeebled by illness.

Keeping this clearly noted matter in abeyance, Biraj enquires, "Golap, is the cooking done? Satu hasn't eaten anything today."

"Almost done, Ma," so saying, the elder daughter-in-law gets extremely busy with pots and pans.

Biraj wouldn't dream of setting foot on the soil of the non-vegetarian kitchen so late in the day,[13] but now there's great urgency. To settle the matter kept in abeyance, she strides over the non-vegetarian soil and moves a little further towards the younger daughter-in-law. In an exceedingly hushed voice, she says, “What do you mean, sitting like this?” She should already have presented herself as a yearning wife to the yearning son, thinks Biraj.

Makhan doesn’t speak. Her head droops still lower towards the ground.

Biraj goes on: “Looking at my son’s health, I’ve no peace of mind, daughter. Don’t you irritate me at such a time, I tell you. Get up.”

Makhan doesn’t raise her face; she says, “What will I do, getting up?”

“What will you do indeed? No one’s asking you to go jigging around. You mustn’t put on such a sour face before my son.” With this, she makes her exit in a huff with a vigorous toss of the head.

Meanwhile, Satu has taken out his hookah that was left behind one-and-a-half years ago. Biraj hasn’t been satisfied with only having done the duty of ordering her two daughters-in-law to prepare his favourite dishes; she’s also had fancy tobacco and tinder brought over to refresh and comfort him, and then, who knows why, got the servant out of the house by letting him off for the day.

Satu briskly stuffs in the tobacco and sits down for a drag. Nitu sits between his outstretched legs and asks, “Where were you, Uncle, all these days?” The boy’s question is one and the same, but not once is his hope for an answer satisfied. Before Satu has managed to make up a fanciful answer about his erstwhile abode, Biraj swoops down from the kitchen and says, “What’s that to you, pest? Buzz off!” She stands Nitu up on his feet, shattering the agreeable cosiness.

Ever unfazed, Satu doesn’t feel the slightest discomfiture at Nitu’s question and his mother’s attempt at a cover-up. He says, “Ah, let him sit”, and he draws Nitu by the hand and sits him down. But by then Nitu no longer has any interest to know.

Biraj begins to fill Satu in on the local news, that is, the birth-death-marriage news of people they know. Satu smokes and listens.

For dinner, the two brothers are seated side by side. Family matters are the most numerous and pressing in a family. While eating, Satu discusses these with his elder brother and mother with sufficient involvement, and confesses unreservedly and at length that it is he who is the cause of the debts that have been incurred. Satish, fixing his eyes at his plate, and Biraj, fixing her eyes on Satu's face, hear his statement about the debts and make no comment on the painful topic.

Satu used to be Bhim-like[14] at eating. But today, seeing him content with so little, Biraj gets upset and says, "How now—not eaten much?"

"The gut's shrunken up, Ma—starved so long. Don't worry, it'll grow again." Thus reassuring his mother's heart, Satu laughs a lot.

The dinner ends quite happily. Stuffing tobacco in his hookah, Satu goes to his bedroom and sits on the bed.

With the plate of rice in front of her, Makhan sits inertly for some time.

In a pained voice, Golap says, "Eat…"

After putting just two morsels of rice in the mouth, Makhan draws back her hand. Golap looks at it once with mournful eyes and doesn't say anything. When a storm rises hundreds of leagues away, waves are said to hit even the windless shores of a sea. Golap isn't unaware of Makhan's mind; the agony of Makhan's heart, as if borne on her breath, is beating against Golap's heart. Yet for once she says, "For my sake, Sister…"

Makhan says, "Sister, get me poison."

With tearful eyes Golap touches Makhan's chin with her left hand and kisses the hand.[15]

"Is my younger daughter's dinner done?" Biraj wants to know and stands close by. For no reason at all it seems to her that the younger daughter-in-law is deliberately stalling.

The elder daughter-in-law says, "Yes."

Looking at the younger daughter-in-law, Biraj says, "Then why are you sitting? Golap will do the washing-up. You clean up and go to your room." As she says this, her eyes fall on the plate Satu has eaten on. The plate was brought away in her presence; but she finds that the younger daughter-in-law hasn't taken her meal on that used plate,[16] presumably because Biraj hasn't been present. It defies description what terrible aversion to the younger daughter-in-law arises within her, and what she feels at this expression of disgust by a wife for her husband. Yet she doesn't raise this matter at all, but says, trembling, "Why don't you speak?"

She herself doesn't clearly know what she wants to hear from her daughter-in-law's lips. There seems to be some reproach somewhere and, driven by her longing for power and authority, she is just desperately looking for some trace of it in the daughter-in-law's words, in order to defang it. But the problem is, there's no way one's voice can be raised over the matter.

After waiting a moment or two, Biraj again says, her inner fury spewing out of her mouth like molten lava, "Still not speaking? You know whose hands you've fallen into? My hands. No one's got away crossing me."

Even then Makhan doesn't say anything, simply because she has nothing to say. The elder daughter-in-law comes forward to intercede and says, "You go, Ma. I'll take her there."

Biraj has no choice but to go. How long can one beat against a rock! Inwardly chewing the younger daughter-in-law's head off, she comes away.

The elder daughter-in-law goes and holds Makhan's hand.

Sitting on the bed and smoking, Satkari is thinking about the incident of the Madhudanga fair—the action and the reaction, and the magnitude of the debacle. Fate was decidedly contrary, otherwise there had been absolutely no possibility of their getting caught. His buddies were all seasoned men. There had been no lapse in exercising caution; they had followed the girl closely at her heels, giving her no inkling of it at all.

Shops and stalls had closed down. Gradually, the fairground had become somnolent and lonely. The kirtan had warmed up well and was in full swing. The lead singer was drenched in sweat, yet wouldn't even think of sitting down. The percussionists seemed to have got into a drunken frenzy.

Outside the crowd of the temple pavilion, the girl sat in a tin shed, leaning against a wooden post, dozing. Suddenly awakened with a start by a furious invocation of Lord Hari, she came and stood outside, perhaps for a breath of air. There wasn't much breeze within the shopping area. Slowly the girl came and stood at the end of the alley.

What happened next happened in a blink of the eye. She was gagged and, at the same time, her body, lifted up in the air, sped off like an arrow.

A large copse close by...full of useful and useless small and big trees, bushes and thickets...But such was the Almighty's disfavour that even in a jungle in the dead of night He'd planted a witness in advance, who got them nabbed by the cops.

Then the court case, the hurly-burly, the innumerable trips, the immense expenditure, and all manner of chaos, and yet each incident so distinct and vivid...

And then the long hard labour in jail. They seem to have squeezed out his body's strength and put it to work. A terrible servitude he's had to endure.

But Satu lets out a sigh not because he's had to endure that unendurable torment. He recalls the girl's face: a treat for the eye, with a tattoo spot on black skin; excellent health; two large eyes; no vermilion or conch-bangles;[17] no second piece of cloth on the body;[18] just a dumb rustic—one glance made this obvious. Who knows whether she had come alone to the fair or had companions? Where she is now and what her plight is—who knows that either!

Satu is wondering about this when, at the sound of the door-bolt, he slowly turns his eyes and sees that Makhan has come. And he also sees that Makhan is prettier than that girl…

“Showed up at long last!” he says. “Come.”

But instead of directly proceeding to the bed like a tamed or spellbound person at her husband’s call, Makhan moves away to stand by the wall. Satu can’t even make out whether she’s heard his amorous, fond invitation.

Unavoidably, a prologue there was to this meeting of Makhan and her husband, but it cannot be said that a confluence of currents had penetrated the fibres of her being. A faint tenderness had been born from association, and this did show up now and then. Above all, Makhan couldn’t deny that a dread lord, sitting somewhere with a sceptre in hand, had drawn her into a union sealed in public. But Makhan came to know her husband. People know people by a smile, a word, a look. And if it is difficult to conceal the nature of soul from soul so acutely intent on knowing each other, then, after the knowing, it’s just as difficult to shut one’s eyes to the knowledge. Yet some contact there was, pleasant or unpleasant. There was an obligation and inducement of duty—even though it was a mixture of the pleasant and unpleasant, and even though between reluctance and willingness, reluctance was stronger. There were hurt feelings; there was a sustained awareness of he-is-I-am…

All these are gone. Like drops of water fallen on the hot sands of a desert, these have disappeared to find refuge, who knows where, in this vast universe.

Makhan keeps her eyes laid on her husband’s eyes. Satu doesn’t understand the meaning of that look. He doesn’t understand that even though they both are humans, their worlds are different, that it is as if an unaccustomed spirit of an unknown world has been brought down in chains to a spirit of this world, that such a look of woman at man is the dazed look of one stunned by horror, a silent scream…

Satu keeps laughing and says, "Some sulk,[19] I say? I'm calling, yet you don't come! Enough of coyness, now come, lay off. Or do I have to get up?"

Lowering her eyes to the ground, Makhan gulps once. Her heart is beating wildly, her whole body is stiffening…

"Ugh!" Venting his annoyance and sarcasm, Satu gets up.

Makhan only keeps shrinking back. She has no awareness of where she wants to go. She has no place to go. Yet she stiffens and keeps shrinking away, as if aiming for the boundless, unfettered world beyond the walls. Her physical being only senses a harsh resistance on her skin. The skin on her back is being chafed raw by the wall's abrasion.

Satu is coming forward…

His touches are piercing Makhan's entire body like venomous stings…

But there's no more room to shrink away. The next moment the whole of her shrunken, stiffened body seems to let out a blast of compressed air repulsing the external pressure, and her entire soul, ignited by a flash of lightning, suddenly blazes up into a huge red fire to make a desperate stand.

Satu sees this—it's impossible not to see such a thing—but he doesn't care. If he had the mind to care, he wouldn't have gone to jail. He says, "Don't they say people can't bear to be happy? No use staring like this! My…"

Seeing Makhan raise her hand, Satu stops short. Makhan's manner of raising her hand is very unusual—its purpose seems to be not just self-defence, but something more sinister, for sure. However reckless a character Satu may be and whatever mistakes he may have committed here and there, this time he makes no mistake. He panics. He backs away saying, "Want to hit—do you?"

Makhan says, "Don't touch me."

"If I do?"

"Better don't."

A shiver runs through Satu's heart.

Immediately he imagines his wife has in her left hand—because he himself frequently has in his own hand—some sharp weapon covered with her sari.

Satu turns back. Running as if for dear life and flinging open the door with a bang he comes out and screams, "Ma!"

Biraj has been awake, of course. The moment her son's frantic voice strikes her ears, she jumps up, responding to his very first call. "What? What? What happened?" Asking anxiously, she opens the door of her room and comes out.

Satu says, "Bring out your daughter-in-law. I won't go into that room. Says she'll kill me."

Biraj bursts out, "Says she'll kill you?"

"That she can. Search her clothes—maybe she has a dagger or something."

At this Biraj loses her head. She has spent a long day in utmost distress. Her nerves, continually strung up and down and rattled with anxiety, have become exhausted and enervated. The worn-out, wasted look of her son has made her sick of everything. To top it all, her blood is still boiling with irritation and fury at having to keep chasing this inhumanly perverse daughter-in-law.

Now this same daughter-in-law has risen to murder her son with a dagger—this sudden news sets the very bones of her skull on fire.

"Where is she?" With this, she immediately charges at her daughter-in-law, crazed and bereft of all sense of good and bad, and of right and wrong.

Her eyes see her daughter-in-law standing in a corner, but not the manner in which she's standing. She doesn't fear knives or daggers but springs forward and lands before her. She grabs her by the neck, and brings her in front of herself; then shoving her by the neck, she brings her to the veranda and down into the courtyard, drags her across the courtyard and, lowering her hand from the daughter-in-law's neck, unbolts the main gate and says: "Go to hell!" With a final shove on her neck, she throws her out of the main gate. Then, bolting the gate, she stands panting.

The sound of the bolt reaches Satish's ears upstairs. He asks, "Who opened the main gate?"

"Ma," replies Satu. And then, very dejectedly and in a lower voice, he says this one thing about himself: "Jail was better for me."

Notes

1. The first section of this story in the original has a title: *Pratham Ghatana*, which perhaps would best translate as 'The Prelude'. However, since no other section of this story has a title, I have agreed to do away with this one as well. Whether I would have been able to bring Jagadish Gupta round to my point of view, I do not know. From what I know of him, he might well have dismissed it as privileging mere elegance over substance.

2. 'Madhu's Heath'. The village adjoining the heath is also known by this name.

3. Two sub-castes of Bengali Hindus.

4. The Swing Festival—the celebration of one of the amorous sports of Lord Krishna and His principal mate Radha. The two sit on a swing, which is rocked by His lesser mates, the Gopinis. Divine eroticism provides an ironic backdrop to the beginning of the story.

5. The narration of Krishna's amorous exploits through songs and gestures, transporting the performers and audience into collective ecstasy.

6. Worshippers of the god Vishnu, one of whose incarnations is the lover-god Krishna. The *Vaishnav*s look upon the latter's exploits as metaphors for profound religious truths.

7. Food sanctified by having been offered to a deity.

8. The supreme mother goddess Durga, embodiment of the primeval energy, worshipped in the form of a magnificently beautiful ten-armed woman mounted on a lion and slaying a demon.

9. In Hindu mythology, the primeval ocean was churned by gods and demons, using the divine snake Vasuki as the churning-cord. It was an awesome event. The churning yielded the lost drink of immortality, *amrita*, and other treasures, but also caused Vasuki to throw up his venom that nearly destroyed Creation.

10. It is an awkwardly constructed sentence in the original. The word 'thought' has been added here as a crutch.

11. That is, his own wife. It would be extremely impudent of him to refer to her more directly.

12. Beef or chicken (even the latter was a taboo in orthodox Hindu homes of the day), perhaps rounded off with an alcoholic drink.

13. Biraj, being a widow, is a strict vegetarian who must purify herself with a bath after coming in contact with anything non-vegetarian. This late in the day, however, she would already have had her bath and so wouldn't, normally, come into this kitchen.

14. Bhim, the second of the five Pandavas in the *Mahabharata*, who is known for his gluttony.

15. Such indirect kissing would be more common than proper kissing between similar people in similar situations in Bengal.

16. As a chaste, devoted wife is supposed to do.

17. These would have been the marks of a married woman; she is a widow.

18. That is, she wore only a sari, no blouse and petticoat, which were then still an urban fashion.

19. Because she has had to live without him for so long.

So Long as the Sun and Moon*

At his father's behest and with his mother's permission,[1] Dinataran has married and brought home his sister-in-law, Prafulla. Not only has the first wife, Kshanaprabha,[2] not died but, moreover, a male child has been born of her womb. The child is just about eight months old.

Marrying twice appears to have become a custom in Dinataran's family. His grandfather Ramtaran and his father Jagattaran both married twice, though after the first wives had ascended to heaven. Thus, marrying a second time is quite a familiar, home-grown practice for them. But this very home-grown practice, familiar for generations, has turned a bit complicated and appeared under a mysterious veil of unfamiliarity in Dinataran's case.

Not much blame attaches to Dinataran. Everyone looked as far as man's foresight could possibly reach. Dinataran looked, too. But their foresight only skimmed over the external aspects of the time to come. No one tried to penetrate the ever-dark minds of others behind the curtain; nor did Dinataran. There was

*Originally published in Bengali as '*Chandra-Surya Jatadin*', in 1929.

only a slight apprehension that it would be a family of two wives. Dinataran's parents thought they'd prevent major trouble by remaining vigilant and exercising control. Secondly, though co-wives, they're sisters. Hence, however peeved and jealous they might inwardly be, the thorns of their jealousy wouldn't possibly prick each other too nakedly every now and then. Besides, the thing called seemliness is not entirely a fiction, after all.

The reason for Dinataran's marrying a second time, with a wife still alive, is his father-in-law's property. If Prafullakumari had gone to another family, half the property would have been gone. Not a little property, too.

Dinataran's father-in-law could see no grounds whatsoever for disagreeing with Jagattaran's proposal. Rather, with great enthusiasm, he returned the message that he, too, had been contemplating this for a long time but, not knowing what the views of the other side would be, had not ventured to broach it. He wrote a good deal more of such things; but since the tears shed by his wife were a zenana matter, he let no one know about it, nor gave it much importance himself.

Swarupchandra's property cackles and lays gold, as it were. That this property should be divided, two parts torn apart to fall on two sides on account of the trifling obligations of a daughter's marriage, is a distressing thought. Swarupchandra could easily envisage a *Kabandha*[3] state for himself, but not this. Moreover, it was also to be taken into account that no dowry would have to be paid for this marriage. He worked out, if a dowry were to be paid, how much money in what time would yield that amount as interest.

Thus, as a result of diverse considerations by both parties, Kshanaprabha and Prafulla have taken the positions of wives of the same husband.

Kshanaprabha's age is nineteen.

Who knows why people coined such a catchphrase as 'past twenty, a maid's a jade'. The saying is in no way true. It's just a proof of how much mischief people's wicked imagination can work. Like many other lies, this lie, too, has become entrenched simply through the vicious circle of being repeatedly told and heard by the partisans of male privilege.

If there's anybody who doesn't believe in the saying, this story needn't concern them for now. Let's speak about only one of those who do believe in it. It's Kshanaprabha.

Kshanaprabha's age is just about nineteen, but she thinks nineteen is all but twenty and, past twenty, a maid's a jade.

Women, however, haven't brazenly marked off a limit to men's youth by coining an inane proverb.

In her mind, Kshanaprabha looks at her husband. Then, in her mind, she looks at herself. In her mind, she checks whether she still has, or hasn't, her youthfulness. Now it seems she has, now it seems she hasn't. A lump of doubt, rising in her breast, keeps oscillating. The alternation of tears and smiles, *Malhar* and *Deepak*,[4] goes on.

At such a time as this, Dinataran marries and brings home the fifteen-year-old sister of this very Kshanaprabha.

Meeting *Didi*,[5] Prafulla meticulously takes the latter's feet-dust[6] and then goes on smiling, as though there could be nothing more amusing than this new relationship that has come about with Didi.

Kshanaprabha looks and notes. Prafulla's youthfulness appears boundless. She, too, gives a little smile.

Kshanaprabha's mother-in-law is present there, keenly observing Kshanaprabha. But something she didn't perhaps expect catches her eye. As soon as she sees that little smile on Kshanaprabha's face, a doubt, knocking at her ribs, grows intensely painful.

Has it been good to do the deed for the sake of the property? She, too, is a woman—how irrepressibly keen the craving for exclusive possession is in a woman's heart is not unknown to her. She also knows well enough how hard it is to forgive anyone who seeks to thwart that craving. But this aspect wasn't considered before. The rush of her husband's spirited arguments regarding the property so confounded her and swept her away with such force that her mind never had the time to think of anything in this connection but the property. At the time it only seemed that excellent provision was being made for Dinataran and his descendants. They would spend their days in royal style.

But now, looking at the two wives side by side before her, her train of thought is reversed. Suddenly her own wife-heart seems to wake up and start reproaching her in a stern voice.

The neighbourhood women come and sit down to compare the looks of the two wives. That the soft bloom of fresh youthfulness is very charming on the naturally radiant figure of Prafulla is absolutely beyond dispute. There are no two opinions about this—indeed, it'd be surprising if there were. Someone looks at Kshanaprabha's face and consolingly says, "The elder wife has a sheen, too. Not that she hasn't any…"

Prafulla sits with a shy face, but Kshanaprabha gets up and goes away. This comparison of looks is very embarrassing. It's true, of course, that the neighbourhood women haven't gathered just to establish her inferiority; still, she can't bear their words.

She's the mother of a child…The awareness of motherhood, suddenly dawning in the wake of this comparative analysis of looks, does serve to cover up the shame of her lack of looks, but at the same time, it awakens an unbearable pain. There was a time when her husband would be gazing at this body, too, with enchanted eyes, and a tingling pleasure would raise goose pimples all over it. Who knows if the intimation of whether that time is still there or is gone would ever have reached her soul; and even if it did, it is difficult to guess what form it would have taken. But the most painful fact is that the person who has shattered her slumber today with such great fanfare, and has so suddenly brought to her soul the news that the time is indeed gone, is her own sister.

But Kshanaprabha's mind doesn't fill with gall. Her eyes fill with tears. Everyone is interested only in this body—the flesh of the body, the skin of the body, the complexion of the body! Nobody's eyes fall on the incorporeal, everlasting elixir she's brought out of this transient body. Her heart feels like bursting with the hurt.

How much use her husband has for this body! The attachment and affection of man and woman by way of and by means of this body is headed only downwards like a projected stone. Like a mark in the water, now it's there, now it isn't.

Immediately upon conceiving the child, she felt a most intimate, unbreakable bond of oneness with her husband, and her heart was bathed in wave after wave of an unending beautiful bliss. With the sudden loosening of that sense of bonding, she's been cast into an unbridgeable void, severed from her stalk, bereft of support. There are no limits to this agony.

Even without judging whether it's sensible of Kshanaprabha to suffer so much distress at the neighbourhood women's idle chatter about bodily charms, this much can be said, that she's lost her head in panic. Although many arguments can be marshalled in support of the ultimate vanity of physical beauty, of how extremely ephemeral youth is, how quickly the body grows stale and insipid, how a son-bearing wife is the real and the best thing, still, it cannot by any means be denied that she herself once took pride in youthful beauty, and had the temptation to lure. She's also aware how youthful beauty can rob a person of common sense and render him blind. Hence the panic.

But, that said, the hurt she feels is not all baseless.

Whether because his face is overgrown with a beard or because he smiles sparingly, Dinataran has come to be known to people as a sound person.

Whether he'll lean towards the vain and short-lived beauty and comeliness of youth or will settle for an exclusive spiritual union with the mother of his son is entirely uncertain. What the natural craving of a woman is; and, in case there are more than one such craving, which of them is more developed, dominant and intent; or which is more poignant and urgent—it is not part of Dinataran's family ethos, any more than it is of countless other people's, to carefully guide his steps with such subtle considerations. It is difficult, moreover, to figure out these things in the constant hide-and-seek of feelings. It is doubtful if a woman herself always knows her mind and can discern these things. But the matter becomes more difficult when two wives are thrown together—one of them a young woman of beauty and charm, and the other, the mother of a child.

Both, Dinataran reasons, are his wives—Narayan and Agni[7] themselves are witness to this. So neither is to be neglected. Both must be equally looked after. There must be no disparity in the clothes and jewellery provided. And there isn't any. But, in this case, the disparity is in their looks and age. The core business of youth Dinataran knows; but the deep oneness that a mother, introverting herself body and soul, claims with a father through their son as the intermediary, has remained unknown to him, as it usually does to a man. And just as, at times, it messes up judgement rather than cause a revolutionary catastrophe in everyday outward conduct, so it does now.

Dinataran's family business is large. He himself keeps the accounts, and it is also his job to see to it that the right thing is done at the right time. Consequently, he is a busy man.

Every now and then, Kshanaprabha sends her son to Dinataran, dressing him up quite meticulously. She apparently wishes her son would make himself all-pervading and knock out from his father's view the entire world with its ledgers and books, goods and godowns, stocks and debentures, courts and cases—just as the little Baman[8] all at once stood up, overwhelming Bali.

But it's not within the child's power to work such a great miracle. Those who take the child to Dinataran often bring him right back. Dinataran has no time to pet him.

Dinataran has no inkling at all that he's passing through a critical test. The one who's aware of this is Dinataran's mother. Subhadra realises that, frantic with the fear of losing her husband, the wife is clutching at straws in utter desperation and hanging on single-mindedly to her own extremely intense love for the child. There are no limits to her trepidation, doubts and anxiety—she's trying to hold on to her husband by offering him the treasure of her child.

Prafulla is alive like a flower, like fresh sap. She wants her sister, too, to join in the fun and mirth. Not that Kshanaprabha herself wears a long face all the time. She, too, takes part in the levity, so far as it becomes her.

What Prafulla does with her Didi's son is itself a wild, riotous affair. It is she who has named the child Ankur.[9] But one day Prafulla's *prafulla*-ness is abruptly cut short. Subhadra pulls her up in a terribly harsh tone. Prafulla thinks she's been reprimanded for no fault of hers. Come to think of it, she doesn't seem to have done any great wrong either. It's just that she has not been able to regard this as an alien household. It's her sister's household, so whatever shyness she had, has passed off in a very short time of stepping in here. By nature she's light-hearted, playful and a chatterbox.

"What's all this laughing for no reason, girl?" Starting with this, Subhadra relentlessly raps out words that are at once scathing and searing.

The newly married girl stiffens with fear and shame, and then sheds copious tears as well. But the reason for Subhadra's harsh scolding isn't the naturally restless, laughing, merry and fun-loving ways of Prafulla. Rather, Subhadra quite likes these. But the fact that Kshanaprabha has filled up with a mute anxiety keeps pricking her heart off and on like a mote in the eye. At times Prafulla's boisterous gaiety feels terribly incongruous and distasteful, and an unsparing self-reproach comes over her. It is the agony of this self-reproach that one day, suddenly defying restraint, bursts upon Prafulla like a bolt from the blue. Prafulla starts crying, her eyes in full spate, and Subhadra walks up to a neighbour's veranda with her grandson.

Even Kshanaprabha is taken by surprise. Until now she, too, has been guilty of many wrongs; many costly lapses like carelessness, inattention, indiscretion, etc. have been noticed in her. Subhadra has spoken a few words of disapproval, sometimes with a smile, sometimes with a serious face, but hasn't exploded like this. Keeping silent for a while, Kshanaprabha says, "Don't cry. Even Ma scolds us so much."

But when Ma scolds it doesn't cause so much crying! Prafulla isn't yet able to feel as close to her mother-in-law as she does to her mother. Moreover, the blow is unexpected.

Prafulla thought she was coming here as Didi's co-wife, and that Didi was everything here. That there might be a person here called mother-in-law didn't even occur to her. So when her mother-in-law proceeds to act like the absolute boss, overriding her Didi, she feels the blow is coming from an unrelated outsider, and for no reason.

Prafulla says, crying, "Didi, send me home."

"Ask him," says Kshanaprabha, and at once goes red, bashfully, like a callow adolescent.

She's nineteen, almost a jade.

Those who've made up this myth know a woman as just woman—they haven't looked at her as an individual, apart from the aggregate. But the greatest marvel is that women, forever keeping quiet, have only abetted the lie directly or indirectly without a protest.

But the body celestial that abides within the sanctum of the mind—that which is of infinite sensibility and to which not even the faintest tremor in the corporeal, physical world can remain unknown—knows that it is unique. Even if there should be another exactly like it somewhere, still it is without a second, there isn't another 'it' in the universe.

As soon as she says "ask him", Kshanaprabha's mind conjures up, even at the age of nineteen, her share of her husband's bed, its dreaming and waking hours, its joys and satisfactions… Memories are so sweet.

She's given up the place, not voluntarily, not on request, but compelled by custom.[10] But she feels inwardly embarrassed, and not just at the sweet memories of that place: her place has been taken over by her own sister, who perhaps pictures her Didi every time she gets in there!

Wiping her eyes Prafulla says, "I can't. You ask him."

"Crazy. How can I?" And Kshanaprabha smiles a little.

Of course, Didi can't do that. For Didi to ask on her behalf would not only be unseemly; if misconstrued, it might turn out to be an ugly offence.[11]

That night Prafulla broaches to Dinataran the proposal of her going to her father's house. And, hearing his reply, she turns her back so resolutely that Dinataran's no-nonsense gravitas, losing its wits, keeps whirling round and round, able to locate neither the honey-comb nor the fire.[12] Revealing two sets of teeth through his beard and smiling gravely, Dinataran says, "Tell your Didi. Whatever she does will hold. She'll persuade Ma."

Pushing her over to Didi is just a ploy to evade the real issue. Now at last she realises that her Didi, too, has adopted the same mean course in saying "Ask him." Such duplicity of the human mind is intolerable. Her body seethes with anger. On the other hand, Dinataran's heart, too, goes pit-a-pat—that the sisters are also co-wives simply slipped his mind. It isn't wise to make one co-wife the boss openly to the other's face. There's no easier way of provoking jealousy, knowingly or unknowingly—that's the hazard of it. Whether Dinataran's anxiety will now pass or remain depends on the response, if any, of the other side.

A little later Prafulla says, "I've asked Didi. She told me to ask *ap-*[13]…you." In Dinataran's brother-in-law phase she called him '*apni*'; now she is having to give up the habit.

Dinataran smiles inwardly a little. Luckily, her wits haven't ripened much…A row was all but on! He says, but this time doesn't even breathe her Didi's name, "You're right. I'll manage all that. I'll persuade Ma, Ma will persuade Baba. How much hassle!" He closes his eyes, as if exhausted by the hassle of persuading so many people.

It's the peak season. Inside the house as well as outside, the burden of work is terrible. There's never an end to the coming and going of people in the office-building and the farm-house. The grass in the barnyard has died, and the dust keeps blowing up. There's a constant rush inside the house because the provisions for entertaining the visitors have to be put together and sent up from here. The two of them and Subhadra are barely managing it between them. If the younger daughter-in-law is sent to her father's house at such a time, the elder one would be hard pressed with her son and it'll be difficult to cope with the work. With this objection, Subhadra shakes her head a couple of times in denial, but finally falls in, thinking, "Let her go and stay over for ten–twelve days. The elder one…"

Everything about Prafulla's journey is settled. The luggage is packed. At his mother's bidding, Dinataran has bought clothes for his mother-in-law and a colourful sari in the current fashion for Prafulla. Approved by both Kshanaprabha and Prafulla, these, too, have been packed in. But all preparations are upset by the very one that was supposed to go. Just after bath Prafulla gets the shivers, and in no time her head begins to throb and a raging fever comes on. The carriage is sent back from the gate.

There's such hectic work at the office. Dinataran used to be so busy he hardly had time for his bath and meals. But now that Prafulla is down with fever, how he makes time in all this bustle for his hourly visits to her is the greatest marvel for Kshanaprabha.

And there's no knowing how one thought leads to another. Even when Dinataran had a little leisure, Kshanaprabha would send her son to him, only to be sent back at once. Dinataran had no time to pet his son. But now!

Maybe this is one thing and that another, the two cannot be compared. This is responsibility; that would be just unnecessary gush. Not doing this would be an offence of dereliction of duty; not so the other. Yet Kshanaprabha's anguish isn't relieved one bit for it. The child is surely no trivial matter. Her husband's whole heart, like hers, ought to fall under its sway and their lives should fuse together. The child isn't merely the embodiment of her husband's gratification...Her husband's body is being regenerated in the eight-part body[14] of this child. Recreating her husband's being, she has gifted the child to him.

Yet it is youth that trumps it all!

Loudly flapping his sandals, Dinataran comes to visit, and Prafulla feels embarrassed. She says, "A pain in the neck." That, however, there's no pain anywhere about her is so transparent that it doesn't even call for a look.

Kshanaprabha smiles, too, and says, "Always like that." She says it as if Dinataran came visiting her just like this. Perhaps Prafulla cannot fathom such deep meanings but Kshanaprabha, having blurted out the words, suddenly turns her eyes and looks away. She feels a slight mortification—maybe the words have betrayed jealousy.

Whether Dinataran came to visit her, too, in quite the same way, Kshanaprabha cannot clearly recall now. Some turbulent wave has snatched her up and has been tossing her on its crest. In the turmoil, her mind has lost its bearings and the times past have become hazy.

Prafulla's fever is in remission; after a lot of persuasion, she has taken quinine. In the afternoon, she's sitting on the veranda with Ankur in her lap. Kshanaprabha is sitting close by, stitching her son's pillow cover.

Prafulla says, "Didi, your son's middle name, Taran, has got to go. Horridly old. Bipattaran[15]—what a name!"

Kshanaprabha raises her face, looks at her and then says with a slight smile, "Tell him." But by then Prafulla is rocking the child on her knee and has started singing:

"O my naughty sweetie pie,
Giggly wiggly sleepy eye..."

Kshanaprabha is smiling at her song-making skill, when, at some sound, both of them lift their faces and they see Dinataran in the courtyard, chuckling.

Prafulla's chatter stops immediately; she draws her *ghomta*[16] further down and keeps her eyes lowered. But Kshanaprabha's face and ears grow very hot; she hastily snatches her son from Prafulla's lap and dashes into the house.

Prafulla looks at her husband, raising her eyes just a little. Dinataran smiles and turns back.

Kshanaprabha has noticed her husband's enchanted look. Also, without a moment's delay, she has realised that Prafulla's blooming youth is not the only reason for her husband's enchantment. It's not Prafulla alone that has stirred these ripples of supreme ecstasy in her husband's heart. The child of her womb also has a part in it.

Just before she looked at her husband, she had shot a glance at Prafulla out of the corner of her eye. No magician, by just endowing the bodily frame with beauty, could have outshone the picture that Prafulla made with the child in her lap. That picture couldn't but catch a man's eye as well.

And when she found her husband keeping his enchanted, hungry gaze fixed on that very picture, she forgot herself in a sudden fit of spiteful repulsion and snatched the child away to deprive her husband of his enjoyment. It is just this image of ultimate union that she's been seeking so desperately.

Fuel is added to the flames the very next morning. Prafulla calls out "Didi", and then, about to say something, stops short. She's too shy to speak, but keeps smiling sweetly.

Kshanaprabha says, "What is it, dear?"

Prafulla says, "Tell you later," and then, just as she's about to turn back, Kshanaprabha grabs the end of her sari and says, "What is it, tell me."

Mere curiosity wouldn't be so vehement. Who knows what Kshanaprabha's thoughts were, but her tone unmistakably conveys the sense that it would be difficult for her to contain herself if there was too much delay.

Prafulla says, laughing, “Nothing…just like that…Oh dear, I forget what I was going to say.”

“Say, or you wish me dead.”

“Okay, let go of my sari.” Gathering up the end of her sari, Prafulla says, “Feeling shy, Didi.”

But Didi’s eagerness by then has become fierce. She says, “Don’t care. You won’t go without saying it.”

Very strange, surely, this desperate insistence of Kshanaprabha on hearing the matter.

Looking at her face, Prafulla says, “You sleep upstairs tonight. He wants a baby by his side.” And immediately she runs away with thumping feet.

But what begins to happen here defies description. Kshanaprabha just gazes into space, sallow and pale-faced, as if Prafulla has sunk her teeth into her heart and sucked out the last drop of blood from her body in an instant.

She can’t figure out the exact words in which Dinataran has expressed his wish. But within her breast, at the soul’s omniscient core where unspoken messages are transmitted automatically, there, everything becomes indubitably known in the blink of an eye.

Her husband has not wanted her with her son. He has desired a child from the other one.

That afternoon’s picture has left an impression on his mind—with somebody else’s child in her lap, its beauty then didn’t come out in full. When will Prafulla show her husband her own child in her lap! Perhaps her husband’s hankering for that day, suddenly awakened, has become truly irresistible.

It seems to Kshanaprabha that her life is a delusion—her hopes, desires, affection are all delusions. Above all, her childbearing is also a delusion. Having got free scope for gratification, having got her, her husband has only played with her. As she keeps thinking, the feeling that rises in her mind is a grievous sin for a chaste wife. Her mind sickens in disgust at the thought of her husband.

It seems to Kshanaprabha that darkness is closing in on her from all sides—not a vast, soothing darkness, this darkness pierces the eye like a sharp spike. She's at the centre of this darkness; those who are prowling all around her are not denizens of this world, they are so monstrous and hideous.

Prafulla wears the beauty-spot, does her hair. The desire for charming her husband seems to brim over her whole body. Kshanaprabha watches with a blank look.

One day, while she's watching, her heart gives a shudder and she, overwhelmed by a sudden fit of frightened love, snatches Prafulla to her breast and melts in a flood of tears. Prafulla sits in silent amazement, not understanding one bit the reason for Didi's strange crying.

But just a little later Subhadra enters the room and, finding tears in the elder daughter-in-law's eyes, sizes up the situation to some extent; and after just a little reflection, the beginning and the end, the cause and the effect, neatly fall into place, and the reason for the crying becomes clear to her.

But Subhadra is all mistaken.

For her, the trodden path that lies with innumerable footprints of people on its breast is the true path, the eternal path, and one may stray from it only to meet with harm at once. That anyone might consider this sanctioned path, which our predecessors have merrily spent their lives traversing, not commodious or comfortable enough, that anyone might not only demand but crave for some other path, is inconceivable to Subhadra. If anyone were to bring any such idea to their lips, Subhadra would call them crazy. So, observing Kshanaprabha's lifeless apathy, she's been attributing it to just her natural womanly hankering for her husband; and now she has no doubt that the source of the latest tears, too, lies there.

But it's all wrong. This isn't why Kshanaprabha was crying.

As she watched with apathetic eyes Prafulla sprucing up, it occurred to Kshanaprabha that this one's lot, too, was like her own. She, too, was mistaking gossamer for bonds of love. She, too, was feeding the ever-mounting hunger for gratification and thinking it the ultimate fulfilment of life. But when the day of reckoning with the soul's hunger would come, and when that hunger would become implacable, then not a trace would remain of this magic dreamland, then she would face a stark void and find the world as lifeless as a corpse. In vain she was adding fat to the fire; the poor thing didn't know that meteors were about to blaze up in her sky.

Prafulla hugs Kshanaprabha with both arms and says, "Didi, dear, are you angry?"

Kshanaprabha doesn't reply. The words that are seething inside cannot be spoken. Lifting sad, misty eyes, she looks at her sister's face…and looks on. She isn't angry. Suddenly, putting out her hand, she touches Prafulla's chin and then kisses the hand.[17] "Where are we going?" she wonders. "Why has this one become my companion?" She thinks and thinks, till her mind loses its way in the boundless, dark, tangled depths of her thoughts, and she hasn't any ability or vitality left to even let out a sigh.

One night, moved by pity, Subhadra brings about a catastrophe.

Kshanaprabha is about to get into bed after dinner, when Subhadra comes and says, "I've got your bed made upstairs, daughter."

Instantly, Kshanaprabha springs to her feet. Some word, or perhaps just a scream, rushes to the tip of her tongue, but only makes her lips tremble; no sound comes out.

The next moment a mute passion fills her eyes.

Subhadra looks in amazement at her daughter-in-law's eyes, trying to comprehend the meaning of her conduct. But, not finding any agreement in any respect between this and her shrewd mother-in-law-ish notions, she flares up and says, "Go."

Kshanaprabha puts a foot forward but remains standing.

Subhadra has come with an unshakable vow: the elder daughter-in-law would be nursing a hurt, of course, but she must be sent upstairs tonight.

Again Subhadra says, "Go."

Picking up her sleeping baby, Kshanaprabha begins to move.

Dinataran is lying down, reading advertisements of pens in a weekly magazine by lantern light. At the sound of footsteps, he turns his eyes.

What his eyes so boundlessly hoped to see when they turned this way, what sight almost made them recoil, and then what thought has made them stay—all that is obvious. Kshanaprabha, too, sees it all with her own eyes.

Presently her feet slowly move towards the bed, but by then all awareness of motion is dead in her mind and body.

Dinataran says, "You've become so thin, I see. Even the baby looks rather thin." Dinataran's entire concern about the health of his wife and son after such a long time blows away in the wind, without leaving the tiniest trace in the world. Getting no reply, Dinataran lines up many effective words of appeasement, and begins to consider what means should be adopted in case these failed to produce a result.

Kshanaprabha lays the baby on the bed and at once suddenly starts from head to foot. She didn't know such a thing would ever happen.

Her body is sickening at the thought of getting into this bed...That man close by is just a mass of flesh, as loathsome as it is gluttonous...His whole carnivorous body is, as it were, just one gaping mouth...It seems as if she gave up touching that body with her mind at some time past remembrance...

Her hand touches the bed and immediately she feels this is her last coming here. She's standing on the last step before the fall. After this...

Kshanaprabha shuts her eyes in terror.

But the god[18] doesn't let go without exacting the tribute due to him.

The dead of night.

Suddenly awakened by a cloudburst, Dinataran sees that Kshanaprabha is not in bed; the baby, too, is not in bed, and the door is open. Dinataran gets up and first looks about the bed, then the veranda, then the courtyard, and then raises a clamour, gathering everyone from all around.

Subhadra's throat is parched dry as wood.

Jagattaran keeps shouting and rushing people in all directions.

Kshanaprabha is nowhere—not indoors, not on the veranda, nowhere around the house.

But she was somewhere, of course.

In the morning, somebody nabs and brings her in, and then stands, turning away his face. Everyone turns away their face.

She is naked now.

And stark mad. But the baby is very much at her breast.

Notes

1. Before setting out for the wedding ceremony, the groom seeks his mother's permission to 'bring a *daasi* (maid)' for her.
2. Jagadish Gupta's choice of names for his characters may sometimes seem deliberate. 'Prafulla' means both 'blooming' and 'cheerful'. 'Kshanaprabha' means 'of brief brilliance' and is one of the names of lightning.
3. A mythical headless monster.
4. Two *raga*s, here meaning something like 'rain and shine'.
5. Elder sister.
6. A common expression for doing *pranam*, which means bowing the forehead down, touching with one's hands an elder's feet and then one's own forehead.

7. Vishnu and Fire: two Hindu gods invoked to sanction a marriage.

8. 'The Dwarf', an avatar of Vishnu that suddenly assumed an immense size and overcame the demon Bali.

9. 'Bud'.

10. When a man takes a second wife, the first one has to understand that she has automatically lost her place in his bed.

11. She might be suspected of trying to manoeuvre her way back into her husband's bed.

12. This roundabout sentence with its thinly-veiled erotic import exemplifies one of the ways in which Jagadish Gupta tackled the social censorship of his day. See 'Introduction', *xv.*

13. '*Apni*', the honorific for 'you'.

14. Two hands, breast, forehead, two eyes, throat and backbone. Alternatively, two great toes, two knees, two hands, breast and nose.

15. 'Bipattaran' means 'rescuer from danger'. With the 'taran' gone, the name would come to mean simply 'danger'. What is going through Kshanaprabha's mind? She has a child; Prafulla, not yet: the child is quickly becoming the focus of the most dangerous crosscurrents.

16. A sari-end worn like a scarf or hood to hide a woman's face from public view; also worn at home in the presence of elders, and even before her husband if others are present.

17. See note 14, 'A Bond Defiled'.

18. *Pati-devata*: 'husband-god', the orthodox status of husband to wife.

Son and Son's Wife*

Akshayananda of Sujatpur has gone to bring back his daughter-in-law, that is to say, the wife of his son Amritananda. The daughter-in-law, Maya, has left, disgusted with her husband; and, before leaving, she made known her disgust in plain language.

The marriage took place a short time ago—not even three months—and so much has come to pass already!

In order to bring his son, Amrita, over to the straight and narrow, Akshay got him married to the beautiful Maya. Amrita's wife Maya's beauty is flawless. The loveliness of her body, the splendour of her figure is boundless like the moon's; the delicacy and symmetry of her features beyond compare. One cannot regard such beauty for long without taking leave of one's senses.

*Published in Bengali posthumously in 1959 as *Putra Ebang Putrabadhu*, adapted from a part of his novel *Gatihara Jahnabi*, published in 1935.

The wedding was at the auspicious twilight hour of a spring day.

Both the families are wealthy, and there was great pomp. But in a realm far above the reach of all spectacle, festivity, laughter and gaiety was enthroned Maya in her resplendent beauty. After the giving-away ceremony, when the priest of the bride's side, Jayram Smrititirtha, said, "Please give your blessing to the bride", and lifted up her veil, the assembly was struck dumb. All noise was silenced and all activity stilled in an instant and the bride's lowered face, exquisitely tender and happy, rose above all the splendid adornments, light, colour and excitement. It was matchless! For a moment everyone felt that in the beauty of her face, the girl had brought in the treasure of the world-adored Lakshmi's[1] ever-flowing blessing, and they were bowing their heads in acceptance. As if in thanksgiving for such beauty, the benediction rose from their hearts: "Be happy, Bride!"

If anyone's actions were to defile such beauty, they also thought, the offence would be unpardonable.

The memory of that day's astonishment,[2] like a scar, is yet to fade away from the minds of many.

But Amrita has no appreciation of its worth. He seems mentally deranged! A beauty that is like the very essence of this earthly life is within his reach, and yet he seems to have no desire to open his eyes and hold it in the embrace of their vision.

His friends are inwardly quite outraged. They fancy themselves in the place of the beloved of a beauty like Maya, and burn in boundless jealousy. They broach the topic, hoping to see some wild, ecstatic jubilation from him over his wife, but Amrita says, "Oh that, how long? Almost dull as dishwater already." And he adds, "Winning hearts, taxing my brain and getting into a tizzy over it goes against my grain."

Friends listen and feel Maya has been banished to an arid and barren wilderness under a brutish husband. Indignantly they give up on the topic; some even let out a sigh.

The coming of Maya has transformed the look of the interior of Akshay's house. There wasn't any untidiness before; there isn't any now, either. But somewhere beyond all this, a fog has lifted from everyone's soul and it seems as if the place is ringing with the clear, sweet melody of *agamani*[3] in autumn moonlight. The glorious, radiant beauty of this autumn goddess is in every part of Maya's body. And having brought in a cornucopia of matchless splendour, provisions and ornaments,[4] she seems just as worthy of adoration as the Mother of the Universe.

Mother-in-law Kalyani feels like keeping the girl clasped to her breast. "My daughter," she says, "is Lakshmi." And it's true—not only in beauty, but also in qualities. No one has a doubt that the most trifling thing or word, touched by her hand or smile, becomes exquisite in content, colour and flavour.

Small children vie to eat on the same plate with her.[5] Even the rice, they say, gains in taste if she just lays her hand on it!

Such is the scramble for her.

But Amrita neither appreciates nor cares about all this.

Which things of the mind are better expressed if kept concealed, which words are better answered if ignored, how an insignificant point might come to be invested with significance for hidden reasons—all such fine discriminations and subtle matters are as completely foreign to Amrita's inner world as the knowledge of scriptures was to Ghatotkacha's.[6] His mind is as devoid of gaiety as it is of delicacy, and, for want of these, his crudity is without parallel.

Maya lies by an edge of the bed—only her two feet are visible at the bed's end. But Amrita never once glances at those two feet. Not once does it occur to him that the person lying motionless under the covers is not quiet in her mind. Countless sparkling dreams are constantly turning up in her young heart like diamonds in a mine, and countless embraces are taking place in those dreams. From morning till now she has smiled so many smiles, thought up so many questions, framed so many answers, unmaking and remaking them...Her mind is now awake, all eyes, waiting and watching over this intricate web of questions and answers.

Amrita cannot think himself to be her beloved. Footsteps of a beloved woman coming to a tryst cannot reach his ears. Maya, having set out on a tryst in her daytime dreams, has now come in the closest proximity of him in the quiet solitude of night. She has visions of woodlands in full bloom, but Amrita can't see them in his imagination. He doesn't have the delicate sensibility needed to decode the subtleties of wait and expectancy.

One day he hammers home how crude and blatant he is.

Already Maya has been feeling not only surprised, but also disappointed at her husband's ways, that is, at his senseless bluster and his zest for the tritest of topics, when, one day, the levels of his education and gumption—his distinguishing features—get exposed.

"Your *dada*[7] couldn't find any other place to flaunt his learning. Written me a letter in English, just to show off! Huh, we, too, know some English," he says, lighting a cigarette.

Although Maya is old enough to feel happy at the glad tidings that her husband knows English, this is not the time for single-minded enjoyment of precisely that happiness. And what's the point of delivering the news of his knowledge of English with such vehemence! Maya doesn't understand the reason and her heart trembles.

She doesn't know that on that very day, this "English-knowing" man was badly humiliated over the issue of knowing and not knowing English. With great swagger he had gone to show his brother-in-law's letter to his friends. Then he didn't see any reason to resent the insolent flaunting of learning by his newly-acquired relative; rather, he felt quite proud that the writer of the letter was among his kin. But who could have known that his friends, instead of being amazed and delighted by the letter in English, would ask him to read it and explain it to them, and he wouldn't be able to do that!

And when his friends saw he couldn't do it, they enquired, "What did you tell your in-laws?"

"What about?"

"Knowing English?"

"Nothing."

"Then why has the gentleman done such a thing?"

"He alone knows."

"Then send back the letter to him, writing: 'Please send it again in Bengali, neatly printing the characters…'"

Hearing only this far and no more of what was being said, Amrita has come back, furious at his brother-in-law, and even now is in no mood to pardon this learned relative.

Not many words—neither harsher than these nor those more appropriate to the moment—are exchanged with Maya. So, he relieves his heart by venting his anger at Ganapati[8] and emphatically proclaiming to Ganapati's sister his own knowledge of English.

Then, after a few vigorous puffs at the cigarette, Amrita fishes out a different topic from his store of not-too-old memories. This topic is pleasurable, so now he smiles and says, "Who's the girl that sat on your left in the *basar* room?"[9]

"My best friend," says Maya, by way of information.

In an elated voice, Amrita says, "Then my best friend, too. Recently married?"

"Yes."

"The bugger," says Amrita, in envy of the man that has married her best friend, though Maya doesn't understand this. And then he smiles a little and asks, "Older than you, or younger?"

"Two months' difference between us. She's the older."

Amrita doesn't ask any more questions, but says, "Nice eyes."

Indira's eyes are beautiful indeed. To call beautiful eyes beautiful in passing or in praise need not be *ultra vires*, even if these eyes belong to another man's wife. But there is something in Amrita's voice which brings tears to Maya's eyes. Maya can't see her husband's face and so doesn't see the look that comes on his face as the body of another man's wife is intimately fondled in fancy. But the tone in which the eyes are praised is enough—there's a heart beating in that tone and the heart is thirsting.

Only Maya knows how her own heart feels—she has no power of speech left in her.

Amrita isn't even aware that he hasn't received an answer. He's lost in his thoughts of the girl. She sparkled with laughter and mirth, and her eyes were lovely…Maya's complexion is brighter, but Amrita thinks there's nothing extraordinary about it. Indira's eyes, on the other hand, are soft and full—so extraordinary that, why, another such pair of eyes can't be found in town. Amrita gets resentful. This one—meaning Maya—is here, sure enough; but why should the other one become someone else's exclusively! Amrita grows sick of life and feels he wouldn't mind if someone were to slit his throat right away.

"What did you chat about with the missus at night, tell us"—Sudhir, Satyen, and all the others press Amrita.

Cocking a brow, Amrita says, "Can't get an answer to my words—how can I chat?"

Sudhir laughs and says, "Got no answer to what words?"

Then Amrita tells them about the girl who is his wife's best friend, whose name is Indira, and whose eyes are proving impossible to forget. And he spices up his thoughts with such fulsome relish that it seems he'd have no regrets if only he had married her rather than Maya. And the rest that he hints at is better left unsaid.

Satyen listens and says, "Billy goat!"

"Why, why, why call me a billy goat?"

"About as bright and romantic! Stupid, can their hearts bear such words? How could you mention such a thing?"

"You can; you only need the strength," saying this, Amrita puts on such a strong expression as if there's no adversary worthy of notice in the world.

But Amrita is utterly surprised the very next day. Not in his wildest dreams did he imagine that the whole neighbourhood would go crazy over just these utterances of his.

Amrita's friend, Sudhir, is also newly married—"newly" in the sense that the question whether it was right to marry hasn't yet arisen in his mind. And he hasn't found anything so charming in another woman's eyes that he'd cast aside his wife and keep planted before him the owner of the exquisite eyes. Amrita has bagged an incomparably beautiful wife, and yet he craves his wife's best friend as an add-on for the sake of her eyes—this, if not madness on Amrita's part, is stuff for gossip surely.

"Our friend's a real connoisseur," says Sudhir.

"Who d'you mean?"

"Amrita. He saw his wife's best friend in the basar room." Sudhir smiles.

Amba realises that the story didn't end with the seeing. So she says, "Spoke about it?"

"Yes."

"Then?"

"Then what? Left his heart there. Amrita has lost his heart and is now running around crying."

Amba comes to Maya and, after repeating these words, whispers in her ears, "Who's this friend, sister?"

The question is just banter, but Maya draws back her face with a start. Maybe in Amba's lighthearted question there was the fault of unwarranted curiosity, that is, meddling, but nothing exactly heart-rending. It is Maya's mind that was in a heart-rending state. Because her mind was already laden with pain over the matter, she can't take the banter. The matter has got around and aroused ridicule, curiosity, snigger and sneer—these are harsh thoughts indeed; but still harsher is the fact that her husband himself has spread this gossip about her best friend. He has humiliated his own wife by saying these dirty things out of lust for his wife's friend. Moreover, she has now been entangled in the gossip in a way that makes it seem as if her husband wanted precisely to demean and disgrace her. Maya suddenly bursts into tears.

At the moment of this tearful crisis for Maya, the mother-in-law appears on the scene and, as she asks to know the reason for her daughter-in-law's tears, the crisis at once turns serious. Having asked that, she keeps eyeing Amba.

Taken aback, Amba can't say anything at first. But Kalyani doesn't let go of her, and under her sharper and sharper interrogation, Amba spills out the entire story.

Kalyani listens and can't help losing her cool and raising her voice at the same time. Of course, she doesn't say anything against Amba individually. She wants to know in general terms why the wives and daughters of the neighbourhood are worrying their heads over other people's worries. Wouldn't it be proper for them to mind their own business and each keep to her own place? And isn't any deviation from this an extremely disgusting indecency?

Kalyani asks many such questions, but having no proper answer to any of them, Amba keeps silent. When Amba finds a chance to get up, Maya, doubly ashamed, is unable to lift her face, and there's no limit to Kalyani's misery at seeing how her son is exposing his true nature to her daughter-in-law.

As the husband of an exquisitely beautiful woman, Amrita has attracted some popular attention—of a good number of both men and women. Hearing about the torments suffered by the newly wedded wife, some of the elderly women of the neighbourhood pay a visit out of compassion.

There comes Haripriya and, calling aside Kalyani, says very confidentially, "I can neither say nor not say this. God knows if it's true or false, but I hear your son found someone in the basar room and fell for her?" As she speaks, her face clouds over with anxiety.

Kalyani says, "How does it matter to you, sister? And how do you know he fell for anybody? He just asked his wife about her friend."

In these parts, there's no one who doesn't know Amrita. So, with an inward smirk, Haripriya instantly agrees and says, "I say the same thing, too. Amrita's just not the type. But then people are talking too much, sister, bitching too much!"

"How can I help if they do? You're one of the people, too! If you know Amrita isn't the type, you could've kept quiet even if they were bitching."

Haripriya is thus disposed of. After dark comes Katyayani. Kalyani disposes of her in the same way and keeps fretting.

Their son lives right in their midst; they know him. They have shed bitter tears thinking about him. To bring him to the right path, they got him married. But it seems he has never before been so much of a scourge, making darkness close in from all sides. A child possesses its mother's heart completely. It's a clear, luminous, heavenly feeling. It's the highest gift of nature, so it must be felt. But today this child seems to be blinding her eyes with the poison spewed by his breath and pressing on her like a monstrous deadweight, stifling all loquacity and raptness of her heart. There is no escape from his hands. Being his mother, she can't help it. But the daughter-in-law! If the daughter-in-law comes to see through the son, what will happen to her and to this family, how to keep him safely under cover—these worries have been constantly tormenting her soul since before the marriage. But today there is nothing left to cover up, perhaps.

Tears come to Kalyani's eyes.

Her daughter-in-law's life has barely dawned; her heart is like a lotus about to open—all joy, light and sweetness of life still hidden in the depths of the future. The unique, sublime moment at which a complete, overflowing self-giving could make her heart blossom in its own element barely came within her reach and then slipped away. This moment is the basis on which the edifice of a never-fading, never-wavering happiness is built, but the alarmed, startled flight of that priceless eternal moment has left a massive, hopeless agony settled all over her daughter-in-law's heart…Kalyani perceives this stark truth with her entire soul, and her woman's heart is on fire.

But more things happen later.

After the visits of Haripriya, Katyayani, etc., the original story continues to spread, growing in luxuriance and foliage, and becoming more and more captivating in the process. Finally it appears before the world in this delectable form: in the basar room, Amrita pulled the girl by the hand; he'd have surely got a thrashing for this, but was let off only because he was still a groom of the basar room and the girl's father is a close friend of his father-in-law; the mark of the girl's sharp nails can still be seen on his right hand, and so on.

Akshayananda becomes tired of denying the matter; it's unending misery for him. But everything about Amrita is an anomaly. Anybody else would likely have hung down his head in such a disgraceful situation, but Amrita's glee and gaiety is redoubled.

"Look, here's the mark of her bite," he says, calling people over and showing the scar of an old cut, and then guffaws uproariously, baring his teeth.

He shows the scar even to the redoubtable Granny of the neighbourhood.

She says, "Shoo, shameless wretch!"

"But you're not a man. How can you know the fun of shamelessness?" Amrita says and winks—as though his fate has credited to his account in golden letters all past and present honours for shamelessness, and the future, too, owes it to him to justify these honours.

"Come, give me a *paan.*[10] You make paan pretty well," says Amrita, sitting on the bed and dangling his feet.

Maya has been folding paan. She lowers her face and glancing at a just-prepared paan, sticks a clove into it. A single ray of sunlight, coming through a tiny slit above, has fallen on one of her earrings. With their gentle oscillations, exquisite flashes of sunlight are bouncing off them.

"Terrific!" says Amrita, "Give me a paan."

Maya gets up with the paan in hand and puts it into Amrita's hand. Promptly popping it into his mouth, Amrita says, "Heard what people are saying?"

The wife, a newlywed, is always nervous, in case people should be talking; she winces inwardly. But the next moment it comes out that people are not talking about her.

Amrita says, "That I messed up your friend's honour—that's what people are saying, hee, hee, hee..." He goes on wagging his head and laughing freely without a care, "Hee, hee, hee..." Maya stares at her husband's face with her wide-open, deep-black eyes. Her awareness, confounded by boundless shame and agony, takes flight into unknown skies far beyond her husband as well as herself.

"Holy Mother, look at the stupidity of people! On the wedding night..." begins Amrita, but, suddenly interrupted, he has to stop talking. Maya sits down and, grabbing his feet with both hands, cries out, "Stop, I'm falling at your feet." Even as Maya bursts into tears, Amrita goes on laughing. The whole affair is just a matter of fun and banter to him. He has no idea where it stabs.

Kalyani's surmise is correct. Maya's heart has become full of despair and pain. But the thought that hasn't crossed Maya's mind, despite the pain, does so that very day after dark.

Kalyani has begun the night's cooking and has called Maya over. Sitting close by, Maya is passing on the condiments and ingredients. "Let's add some more salt? Will so little coriander paste do?"—through such questions, Kalyani is indirectly training Maya.

At this time, someone calls from the courtyard, "Ma?"[11]

Hearing an unfamiliar female voice, Kalyani turns down the fire and comes out. A shadowy figure is standing in the dim moonlight.

"Who are you?" asks Kalyani.

The woman says, "You know me, Ma. I'm from the Bagdi[12] village." She keeps wiping her eyes with the end of her sari.

Maya comes and stands beside Kalyani. The woman asks, still crying, "Who's this married girl?"

Kalyani says, "My son's wife."

All three then fall silent. Kalyani gets annoyed as time is going by for no reason—the fire is burning away idly; she says, "Landed up and started crying for no rhyme or reason! What's the matter with you? Why are you here?"

The woman says, "I can't take it anymore, Ma. Save me."

Kalyani's confusion and astonishment is suddenly dispelled and her heart gives a flutter. A streak of lightning, as it were, flashes out and by its harsh light she glimpses everything. She makes not the slightest mistake in figuring out why the woman has come crying at such an odd hour, and has come to this very house rather than any other. As soon as she grasps this, she shoots a glance at Maya out of the corner of her eye and suddenly puts on a show of great temper. She cries out, "Why this nuisance at my door? Go away, go away…" She keeps waving her hands so fast as if she would blow the woman away with the wind of her hands!

The woman thinks coming here, too, has been a mistake. "Going," she says and turns back. And as soon as she turns back, the catastrophe that neither Kalyani nor the woman were prepared for in their wildest dreams happens in the blink of an eye. Maya rushes out and grabs her hand and says, "Tell me what you came to say."

The woman stares in amazement at Maya's face.

"Tell me," says Maya, and keeps pulling her back.

"No," says the woman, and, immediately slumping to the ground of the courtyard, starts crying in such a way that it seems she just wants to end her life crying.

In the wild turmoil of her soul, Kalyani desperately keeps calling Maya, "Daughter, come away," and maintains a fiery frown so that even in the dim light Maya might notice it and feel scared.

But her hopes and efforts prove futile. Softly Maya says, "I'll come, Ma, let me hear this. You are trying to cover up in vain. I've understood it all. Still, let me hear."

In Maya's calm voice, Kalyani has a face-to-face experience of how unshakably firm one can be without getting angry and without shouting, and at the same time, shaking up another person. Kalyani stands aside. She wishes she could slit the throat and annihilate the very faculty of speech of this female from the Bagdi village that has come up addressing her as "Ma."

And then, sitting on the ground of the courtyard, Bhuban tells Maya everything. She doesn't even conceal the stain on her own birth: it is this stain that has provided the opening for the persecution.

And she tells everything else, too: Amrita's doings in their village; how many lovers he has there; his yen for her and the immense nonchalance of her lame, invalid husband; her refusal and then being tricked into a room and being locked up there by an intrigue of the girls of the village itself; enter Amrita; her scuffle with him and her flight; and then her coming here with her complaint…

Sitting very close, right in front of Bhuban and fixing her unblinking eyes on her face, Maya hears everything. Standing nearby, Kalyani perhaps hears a little and not the rest.

Even after this, Maya remains sitting.

Going into the kitchen without a word, Kalyani finds that the wood fire has died out and everything has run cold.

Bhuban says, "Let me go. Now you've heard it with your own ears, missus?" But looking at Maya's bloodless, pallid face, she, too, remains paralysed for a while, as if in a trance.

Maya says, "Good I've heard it. Okay, you may go now."

Bhuban goes away. From inside the kitchen, Kalyani orders in a solemn voice, "Daughter, take a bath. You've touched the Bagdi female."

Maya says, "Yes," and then feels like saying, "Mother, how many baths, in how much water, can purify your son?" But she doesn't say this; she doesn't say this out of disgust, out of distaste for waste of words.

After this, the atmosphere of the house turns ominous. And the most terrible thing that comes about is that Maya is severed from the family like the head from the body of a sacrificed beast, and she takes refuge in bed. Every now and then Kalyani shuts her eyes, as if searching herself in this self-created darkness.

Akshayananda, learning about the foregoing developments, draws in a lot of air and lets out just one sigh.

When he hears that Bhuban went to his house to complain, Amrita doesn't come home that night—not, of course, in fear of anyone, but exasperated that there should be such a nuisance to happiness as home. Next day, too, there's no trace of him.

When, on the third day, he makes his appearance, the matter is partly over; that is, Maya is by then in her father's house. For full two days she didn't touch even water. When Akshay saw a live creature was starving to death right in front of him, he sent her away to her father's house.

Learning the facts, Amrita says, "Whew! What temper!"

Akshay, with his helpless mind in a whirl, lays the blame on his daughter-in-law. She has badly disgraced him, demeaned him in the public eye. When he sent her off to her father's house, refusing to take responsibility for her life, he had no qualms about considering her a nuisance. Having himself taken the initiative to hastily dispatch her to her father's house, he keeps imagining that it is Maya who has contemptuously spurned them. He sees immense wilfulness and arrogance in the way she ignored the sympathies of her father-in-law, mother-in-law and neighbours, and their earnest entreaty that she take food and water. A disdain for them as well as a distressing tendency to humiliate them is also espied in her. She has left, creating a scandal. If she were a little accommodating and had stayed back, it would have saved his face.

Akshay becomes angry, but not Kalyani. Her mind's sky is suffused with a glowing memory of her daughter-in-law. She never found the slightest aberration or perversity in her conduct. At every step she found evidence of a refined, decent and gentle heart. Some lapses she noticed, of course, but no offence. She never encountered any evasiveness or duplicity, was never crossed by her, nor disappointed in her as a daughter-in-law. A thousand times, with a start, she would silently bite her tongue.[13] There was no respite in her efforts, day and night, to keep her son's true nature from her daughter-in-law's eyes, and her mind would hurt constantly. Great was the suffering, unforgettable.

And this, too, Kalyani appreciates, that her own womanhood hasn't been content with just maintaining a wifely devotion but has always longed for a certain respect in return—a respect for her purity and individuality; a respect that is not fake or a pretense; a respect independent of fear, lust, greed, piety, pity, censure or praise; a respect of equal for equal; an admirer's respect for an embodiment of sweet tenderness…

But the daughter-in-law has left utterly humiliated; she has received terrible wounds.

After some time, when the turmoil of the events has subsided, it comes to Akshay one day that he has been guilty to his daughter-in-law exactly to the same extent that he has been powerless with his son. He also feels that the longer the daughter-in-law stays away from their midst, the greater will be his guilt. It is also not untrue that he is fond of his daughter-in-law.

So, he sets out to bring back Maya.

Kalyani doesn't prevent him. But she has known Maya. This isn't a girl who'll come back as soon as she's called. If Kalyani were more egocentric she would perhaps have nursed a hurt;

but Kalyani cannot look upon her daughter-in-law as being outside of, and divorced from, Kalyani's own status and dignity as a man's wife. Every woman is placed identically as a man's wife, subject to the same norms in all cases.

Beyai[14] Rasik is a childhood friend of Akshay's, which is a great advantage. There won't be too much embarrassment with him, thinks Akshay. Still, he doesn't send word of his coming, for although Rasik is a good and harmless man, there's never a want of wicked counsellors.

It's because they are childhood friends that Rasik hadn't made enquiries before the wedding. Moreover, he had believed that a gentleman's son would be a gentleman, too.

Having learnt his lesson, whatever mood he may be in now, it should be possible to pacify him—feeling self-assured with this idea, Akshay sets out.

And receiving an appropriate welcome, Akshay is satisfied.

In the afternoon, after a sumptuous lunch and a brief siesta, Akshay says, "Let's go inside and find out. You've no opinion at all, I see! Tomorrow is the eighteenth—a propitious day. I'd like to return tomorrow itself."

From the cordial words and courteous manner of the two beyais it cannot even be sensed that such a terrible storm has ripped through in the mean time.

At the mention of Akshay returning the very next day, Rasik says, "You've just come, stay a few days."

Akshay might have replied in jest, "Why a few days? For such heavenly meals in your house, I could stay a few months!" But he can't say this. He's become laconic in the wavering uncertainty of the atmosphere he's caught in. His mind is distraught. Rasik somehow appears strangely unconcerned: he has mouthed a good deal of irrelevancies, but hasn't at all raised the matter of his daughter and son-in-law.

Akshay says, "That—next time. Let's go."

Rasik and, behind him, Akshay go and stand in the courtyard. Akshay goes a few steps forward and calls, "Daughter, listen."

Maya comes out and stands. Looking at her, Akshay begins, "I'm so happy, Ma, to see you. God knows how your mother-in-law and I myself have suffered since you came away." Then, letting out a sigh—that is, presenting evidence that the suffering is real and still existent—he says, "Then I thought my Ma's goodness is as great as her beauty. How long can she remain angry? She must come again to take care of her son…"[15]

Lightly uttering these endearments, Akshay looks once at the curtain, behind which is his *beyain*,[16] and once at his beyai's face. That side is invisible; on this side are no feelings manifest on his beyai's face—as if he is watching a play in the manner of a disinterested third party.

Faced with such stolid detachment, Akshay suddenly feels everyone has misunderstood and deserted him; he is totally helpless; his only support is this girl; these are outsiders, the daughter-in-law is his own; if only she takes pity…

Now Rasik speaks. He says, "Our position is simply that we won't stand against our daughter's wish. If she wants to go—fine; if she doesn't, then, too, we have no objection."

Akshay listens to these words, pricking up his ears. Then, unnecessarily wiping his brow once with the back of his hand, he frantically says, "Daughter, we'll go tomorrow."

Maya says, "I won't go."

It seems an arrow has gone through his heart. "What?" The pain and surprise that rings out in the monosyllabic word defies description.

Maya says, "Please come to take me the day he becomes good, not till then."

After saying this, Maya comes up and bends down to take his foot-dust[17] by way of taking leave, but Akshay springs back, saying, "No." He's no longer prepared to even grant her the dust of his feet.

Maya slowly goes up into her room. Looking at Akshay's face, Rasik does feel some pity and says, "Come."

Akshay walks, but as if in a trance. To say that he's offended would be saying nothing at all; even to say that he's heart-broken would be saying too little. He feels as if the presumption he had proudly nursed since birth, and assimilated into his life and being, was now going through its death throes, writhing and bleeding as it were, inside his heart. Not only has his pride and joy at being a man living in human society as father of a son, father-in-law of a daughter-in-law and husband of a wife been shattered, but even the awareness that he's a human being has been burnt to ashes in an instant by an intolerably hot breath of air.

The two go and sit in the drawing-room. The servant brings in the hookah; Akshay doesn't touch it.

Rasik says in a dejected tone, "I'm helpless, Brother."

Akshay doesn't speak. Rasik watches his preparations for departure with sad eyes. At one point he speaks out, "Stay back for today, Brother."

Akshay simply says, "No."

Akshay returns home. Many people return from their relative's[18] place. And from other places, too: from the cremation ground after an ultimate loss, from the law court after losing their all to others. Still, it doesn't seem as if they had exited the limits of normalcy. They don't return surrendering their humanity at the door of disgrace. But this is what he's done.

After coming back, Akshay sat in the drawing-room; he lies down right there.

The servant has broadcast the news of his return inside. He brings the hookah and informs him, "Babu, Ma's calling."

"Coming," Akshay says and gets up. As he steps out, he feels his feet are refusing to move.

"What happened?" Kalyani asks, pointlessly. Akshay stares at his wife's face, saying nothing, and then starts walking past her towards the bedroom. Having gone some distance he says, "Daughter hasn't come."

"I didn't expect she would, either."

Akshay stops and says, "You're on her side, I see. But who pays the price of the humiliation I had to bear?"

"Bear because of whom? Day and night, your son is humiliating you and me—who will you ask for its price?"

Deeply hurting, Akshay says, "I'll die," and goes up into the bedroom.

Kalyani comes in to make sure he is well, and finds him sitting in a chair, looking truly lifeless. She asks, "Are you well?"

"Sure."

"What happened there?"

"Puppet dance![19] Daughter-in-law said: 'I won't go.'"

"Her parents were willing?"

"Don't know for sure. Maybe."

"Don't be so upset. Try to understand the whole thing. I'm not feeling upset at all."

"Maybe you're the lion-riding Durga's[20] avatar—little things don't move you," Akshay says and turns away his face. Kalyani only smiles a little at this needless taunt.

The one regret of Akshay that rises above everything else is that his secret sighs have remained real and heart-rending only to himself—no one else in the world has cared to understand him, not even his wife. That he regards his daughter-in-law as the quintessential Lakshmi is very much a living truth. He is extremely fond of her—so fond that he could scarcely bear to see her put her feet on the earth. Having cast his son out of his mind, he had long ago set up for himself an ideal for the girl he'd bring as his daughter-in-law. Having Maya as a daughter-in-law satisfied his desire for a daughter on the one hand, and his craving for that ideal on the other, and he even conveyed all this through gestures and hints. And yet no one has been able to understand him—neither wife nor daughter-in-law.

Akshay languishes in his suffering and remains furious with everyone.

Kalyani, though, takes a different view. She finds no reason to be sorry that her daughter-in-law hasn't come back; rather, with a happy feeling of release, she wishes Maya well. She wrote off her son long ago—he being what he is, the dignity and honour of the family would anyway have to be considered and protected, regardless of him. Kalyani feels that in this respect, too, her daughter-in-law has done the right thing. It wouldn't have been proper for her to come back; for if she did, all of them would have to descend immediately to a level of sordidness from which no one could have rescued them. They haven't fallen out of the decent category—their daughter-in-law is holding them up by leaving them. She has left her husband, their son—in this there's no threat of their turning into social outcasts. If society should ever take it into its head to ostracise them, it would do so being unable to endure the conduct of their son, not of their daughter-in-law. May this chaste girl live forever.[21]

Akshay's heartbreak, needless to say, has become public knowledge. His daughter-in-law hasn't come back; many realise it is their neighbourly duty to offer sympathy and salutary advice in his distress, and a few turn up towards the afternoon.

Akshay doesn't condemn anyone; he only laments that it is truly difficult to size up human beings, that being born a man was the harshest tribulation ordained by fate for him, that this is the source of all his miseries, and that he'll pop off soon.

What most of them say on hearing this are similar in tone and content, apposite to the time, and prescriptions appropriate to the situation. Only Akrur Datta proves different. He says, "You should've married him into a family that understands nothing, feels nothing. A matching family isn't one just equal in means; there must also be parity in refinement of character. Your son has demeaned you enough. If even a fourth of what we hear about him is true, then it's difficult even to receive him as a guest, let alone establish relations with a decent family through him. You fixed the marriage in great secrecy. If I were present during the negotiations, I'd have opposed it."

The words strike Akshay as very harsh. These are not words of sympathy but are glaringly true, and Akshay cannot stomach them. He groans out, "Now don't rub salt into my wound."

"Then give up your son, and give up any hope of your daughter-in-law. If you feel you were humiliated at your beyai's house, blame yourself for it." With this, Akrur Datta gets up.

Blindly and stubbornly, as if bracing for a quarrel with someone, Akshay cries out: "Again—I'll get my son married again!"

Notes

1. The Hindu goddess of prosperity and domestic welfare, represented as a woman of great, mature beauty.

2. Here the original uses the expression *bismrita smriti*, which would translate as 'forgotten memory'. Since this looked like an oxymoron, I have treated '*bismrita*' as a misprint and hazarded in its place a guess, '*bismita*', meaning 'astonished'. However, given Jagadish Gupta's unconventionality, 'forgotten memory' is not entirely impossible, especially in view of the subsequent simile of a 'scar'. On either view, of course, the sentence is an extremely awkward one—an example of the nightmares his translator has to be constantly prepared for!

3. Carols sung in welcome of the supreme mother goddess Durga on the eve of Durga Puja, the greatest festival of Bengal, celebrated in autumn. See also note 1, 'A Bond Defiled'.

4. Maya has clearly brought in a sumptuous dowry.

5. An expression of affection, quite common in traditional households, especially a few decades ago.

6. A character in the *Mahabharata*, half-man, half-demon, of immense size and brawn.

7. An elder brother. Sometimes shortened to '*da*', it may also be used to address some unrelated older males.

8. Maya's elder brother

9. 'Bridal chamber'—where a couple spends their first night and where, before that, women gather around them for a session of revelry, banter and practical jokes.

10. A chewing quid made of betel leaf artfully folded to contain fine-chopped betel nut, lime and other ingredients, and sometimes pinned with a clove to hold it together.

11. A common way in which women might be addressed—especially, as in this case, an elderly woman of a high caste or class by people of the lower orders.

12. An untouchable caste. Upper-caste men may not touch women of this caste, but can have sex with them.

13. Equivalent to saying 'Touch wood'.

14. The father-in-law of one's son or daughter.

15. That is Akshayananda himself.

16. The feminine of beyai, that is the mother-in-law of one's son or daughter, in this case Maya's mother.

17. See note 6, 'So Long as the Sun and Moon'.

18. The Bengali word used here is *kutumba*, which denotes those with whom a relationship has been established through a son's or daughter's marriage. There seems to be no equivalent of it in English.

19. What is actually meant here is almost surely 'theatrics'.

20. See note 7, 'A Bond Defiled'.

21. This stilted-seeming expression actually echoes and ironically *reverses* the standard blessing routinely given to women by elders: 'May you be chaste and faithful' (whereas for men it is: 'May you live a hundred years'). A truly chaste Hindu wife aspires to die married, and so does not wish for, nor is wished, a long life, but in effect an earlier death than her husband's.

Krishna's Consummation*

I was friends with Ranu, but one day we suddenly broke up.

Ranu was young; I was young, too. She was seven, I was fourteen. A senior isn't necessarily the better; still a senior does, perhaps, have certain natural responsibilities towards a junior, especially if they're neighbours.

Towards Ranu, too, I had my responsibilities—to see she didn't come to bodily harm, and so on. Recognising the importance of my status as a guardian, I sometimes tried to discipline her; but trying to describe how far this resulted in her rectification would be as superfluous as dilating upon her beauty. Looking at my serious face, she would roll all over me laughing, and say, "Big boy Kanu-*da*.[1] How he scolds me. Hee, hee, hee…" But I never lost my zeal.

Ranu's father, Jadugopal Datta, was neither affluent nor penniless. There were extra earnings in his job. This was filthy lucre but, with the family expenses covered by his meagre salary, the whole of this filthy lucre got saved.

Births, deaths, passing and failing exams, ups and downs of income, weddings—apart from such commonplace domestic changes, nothing noteworthy usually happens in the homes of

*Originally published in Bengali as '*Aruper Ras*', in 1929.

Bengali householders, nor happened in ours. I failed my exam once, passed it once, and left to fate how I'd do the next time. Jadugopal Babu's salary rose by four rupees; another raise was imminent.

Ranu became ten, I became seventeen.

Entering my study and putting a finger on the death-scene of Nelson in my textbook, Ranu asked, "What picture is this, Kanu-da?"

"Picture of a battle. This man's got a bullet in his chest and is dying from it," I said and, pointing to the dying Nelson with my right hand and putting my left arm around her waist, I looked at her face.

Shooting a swift glance at the door behind and freeing herself, Ranu said, "Show me what other pictures are there."

The significance of her quick glance at the door couldn't be lost on me. And easily as I saw through it, my amazement knew no limits at the precociousness of this ten-year-old girl. But what mischief possessed me I don't know; I said with an amused smile, "There are lots of pictures, but first tell me—you've come to look at pictures or with some other purpose?"

I thought Ranu wouldn't be able to catch the meaning of this roundabout question; and yet I was in suspense, too, to find out if she would.

Ranu didn't answer the question at once. She stood silent for a while and then, suddenly turning to go, said, "I came because I heard you were sitting with a bowlful of *rasagolla*[2] for me. Looking at pictures was a sham."

"Come, have rasagolla, then," I shouted.

But Ranu, too, was then shouting, "Radha, dear, do come over once in the afternoon. We'll stitch a cover for the doll-box." Her shouting drowned out mine. My suspense had been resolved, but an inexpressible humiliation of defeat put me out and darkened my mood completely. The matter had been mere banter, but suddenly turned ugly.

Two days later, Ranu came and informed me, "Kanu-da, it's my wedding."[3]

"What do you mean?"

"Yes, honest. Tomorrow, they'll come to inspect me."

There was no reason for surprise at the news. A change like marriage constantly takes place in Bengali life—to some at a young age, to some at an old age and to others at middle age. Only in Ranu's case, this commonplace change would come about in her tenth year.

I asked, "Who to?"

"Don't know. Baba and Ma are very busy. How many dishes are being made! I just ate."

My mouth began to water. Ecstatically I said, "Bring a little, let me eat, too."

"I'll bring," she said and went off.

She brought a bowl hidden under her sari and, pushing it up to me, said, "Eat!"

I looked at her face in surprise. She had said, "Eat!", but there wasn't the slightest hint of invitation in her voice. Rather, I sensed a thrust in the opposite direction. Why such sudden anger?

I hadn't looked at her face when she was going, but now I noticed every line of her face had hardened.

Ranu said, "Why don't you eat?" Her voice sounded harsh.

"Why did you give it angrily? Can anybody eat if the food is angrily tossed at him?"

Ranu made no reply. With a chuckle, I said, "Oh, you were caught filching, is it?"

"I didn't filch. I asked for it."

"Then why were you angry, serving a brahmin?"

"Angry—when? I just told you to eat."

Pushing the bowl back towards her, I stood up. I felt angry, too. What's all this frowning about?

A dog lay in the courtyard. With swift steps Ranu went down and, turning over the bowl, poured out before it all the sweets—made from milk, thickened milk, curdled milk and cream—and went home crying.

The break-up that I have mentioned earlier started with this incident.

Ranu's looks and accomplishments will be inspected. I go to watch. My eyes first fall on a torso whose face is hidden behind smoke. There's no let-up in smoking. When at last the unrelenting billows of smoke disperse, I see a grizzled, portly, middle-aged gentleman stretching out his hand, proffering the hookah to Ranu's father.

A mat has been spread on the veranda. On it is sitting Ranu's father with the humility of a bride's father; the other man, whatever his relation to the bridegroom, is sitting with his head held high like a bossy figure of the groom's party. And a lad of my age, face lowered, cannot for the life of him be done with his scrutiny of the weave of the mat. I realise this one is the informer, who will secretly report the looks of the bride to the groom.

The boss of the groom's party says, "The girl will be chosen for sure. Even if she's not quite as much as we've heard, she must still be beautiful."

Jadugopal Babu says, "In very good health, too—my Ma."[4]

"Must be. An only child, this girl. Must have fed and filled her well. It's just for want of diet that the females of this land are shrinking in size. The children they bear are shrinking in size, too." So saying, he, too, seems to shrink a little in size, broken-hearted.

Jadugopal Babu says with conviction, "Rightly said, sir, no doubt about that. I think, shrinking and shrinking, the Bengali race will vanish off the face of the earth one day."

But I feel like laughing out. The burden of an unmarried daughter is an undoubted adversity. This bride-inspection ceremony is a part of this whole burden but an exceedingly vital part, since on it depends the deliverance from the burden. The bride's father, his heart fluttering with suspense and apprehension, glances now at his daughter's face, now at the inspector's, and now scans his daughter's features, now looks for the inspector's favour. Even if a bride's beauty should be such as to stand comparison with a golden idol, her father's heart at this time must be parched and quaking. Yet the tragedy of life is so grotesque that precisely at this time, when the mind is sore, he has to repress its violent rebelliousness and mouth sweet words in profusion, clothing flattery as politeness. The exercise, though agonising, is still rather comical underneath.

Anyhow, the boss says, "Same holds for men, too. Think they can eat their fill? Pooh!"

I don't know if Jadugopal Babu has done any thinking on the matter but his eyes bulge out in amazement, as though for the first time now he's suddenly received, from the boss's mouth, the news of the half-fed plight of Bengali men. Mournfully he says, "No, sir, there are plenty of men who the year round, so to say…"

Perhaps he was going to say "starve", but the boss doesn't allow him to proceed and says, "Getting late. No need for too much decking-out, ask her to be brought in just the way she's at home."

Jadugopal Babu, now recalling his own sad plight together with the sad plight of Bengali men in general, becomes still more dispirited and says, "Girl of a poor family…What do we have to deck her out with, *beyai*!"[5] Then, raising his voice, he says, "Maid, are you people ready?"

From inside the house, the reply comes, "Yes."

Beyai—so this is the groom's father himself.

A little later, as the maid leads Ranu up to the doorway by the hand, I look in that direction and suddenly blurt out, "Lovely!"

A wide-bordered red sari over a white chemise, a red silk ribbon tied in a knot on the head, hair braided across the forehead, *alta*[6] around the feet, a tiny black *bindi* between the two eyebrows—Ranu's sprucing up for the inspection is simply this. Yet in this very ordinary make-up, her beauty appears infused with an extraordinary, new sweetness to my eyes.

Turning his eyes from Ranu's face to mine, Jadu Babu's beyai says, "Lovely, indeed. Come, Ma, come, sit." So saying, he places his hand on the vacant spot before him. Ranu slowly comes down and sits before him with a lowered head; the maid sits, face turned sideways, sidling up close to Ranu's body.

But words are at once smothered in my heart. A vague, indeterminate craving, like a veil of fog looming up at a great distance, begins to tarnish my mind's sky. Suddenly I am jolted out of my trance and hear the beyai saying, "Your daughter has auspicious features and she's beautiful indeed—as not usually seen. She's a hundred times more beautiful than I heard before coming. One can have no idea of such beauty by just hearing about it. I'll take this girl." So saying, he holds up both hands of Ranu.

Jadugopal Babu says, "Your immense kindness."

"Not kindness, interest. Your daughter's luck will make a king of my son."

Jadugopal Babu smiles, or rather perhaps "smiles" isn't the right word: his heart's joy and pride seem to brim over under the pull of the beyai's effusive tone.

Inwardly I, too, agree with the boss's words with all my heart. There's no mistaking at all that he who'll marry Ranu has a king's luck and will take home a royal treasure by mouthing a couple of mantras.

After humming and hawing for some time, Jadugopal Babu brings up the issue of dowry. "I'm terribly poor," he says, "waiting with just the girl. Even the means for her send-off…"

The beyai hurriedly bites his tongue, as if Jadugopal Babu has said something shameful and unworthy of his ears, and says, "God forbid! Don't you utter such a thing. I'm taking home Mother Lakshmi[7] herself; she will fill my house with wealth and sons. I'm not after the one or two thousand of yours."

At this, I don't know why, even my eyes fill with tears. This unbearably good news is absolutely unexpected for Jadugopal

Babu. Fixing his gaze for about a minute on the beyai's face, Jadugopal Babu suddenly throws himself face down on the latter's feet. This calamity is absolutely unexpected for the beyai as well. Had he known that his words would land him in such a predicament, he would perhaps have conveyed by post, rather than in person, his noble intention of accepting the goddess of kingly affluence without a dowry. He's a fat man; moreover, an entire human body is prostrate on his feet. It's beyond his powers to readily back away or stand up—he doesn't even attempt any of these. Grabbing Jadugopal Babu's shoulders with both hands, he almost heaves Jadugopal Babu up from his feet and says with a displeased face, "What a thing you've done, beyai! Why d'you embarrass me before your daughter, and why those tears in your eyes?"

I glance at Ranu's face. I've seen her anger, crying, disobedience, naughtiness; but it is the first time that I witness her bashfulness, this exquisite play of colour. Like the rising sun's sanguine glow on hilltops, above all the mist and haze of the lowlands, these first bashful blushes of hers light up the summit of my inner world.

Why he has done such a thing, why he has embarrassed his beyai in front of his daughter, why there are tears in his eyes—Jadugopal Babu doesn't answer any of these questions. Pushed up by his beyai, he sits upright and says in a thick voice, "It's my daughter's great fortune she's going into the family of a great soul like you. Ranu, bow to your father-in-law's feet, Ma."

One could see only the fine, dark curves of Ranu's eyelashes. Presently she lifts her eyes to look at her would-be father-in-law's face. Then, lowering her eyes, she stretches out her hand and touches his feet. Inaudibly he mutters, perhaps his blessings, and tells the maid, "Take Ma inside. The inspection's over."

The maid, holding Ranu's hand, takes her inside. Ranu's hair, spread on her back, is once tossed by the wind. I catch a glimpse of the glow of alta on her feet. A whiff of a sweet scent comes to my nose.

I understand everything—except only why Jadugopal Babu's beyai gobbled up so much sweet in the name of a "sweet snack". That informer, too, guzzled a lot.

Perhaps on the orders of her parents, Ranu has stopped coming out of her home and has become a rarity. Fine. Gallivanting doesn't become a girl who'll go to her in-laws' house in three months' time. But why on earth have I become her *bête noire*? Even after long reflection, I can't figure out the reason. She's stopped talking to me altogether; if we meet, she goes away, turning aside her face—as if we don't even know each other by face. One day, finding her within reach by chance, I grip her hand. At this she suddenly bursts into tears with such a howl that I have to let go of her hand and beat a hasty retreat.

Right from her childhood, a Bengali girl does feel shy at the mention of marriage, and then, however young, she puts on a peculiar air of gravitas the moment her match is fixed. But it's not that Ranu is acting shy with me because I'm an alien male to her now,[8] nor is she still angry, having felt insulted over that day's incident concerning the sweets! For shyness or anger is one thing, disdainful avoidance entirely another, and it's impossible to mistake one for the other. Refusing sweets dished out with an angry face can't have been so big an offence against a nine- or ten-year-old girl that she's not able to forget it at all…Anyhow, cursing her for her obstinacy, I vow not to speak to her unless she speaks to me first.

Daughter being married off without a dowry: at the news of such enormous good fortune of Jadugopal Babu, the eyes of his relatives, neighbours and well-wishers pop out of their heads in excitement. Another consequence of it is that those who are fathers of girls begin to hope that a wind of change is blowing across the land and they'll no longer have to take to the loin-cloth after their daughter's marriage.

At such a time, Ranu one day breaks the ice with me.

"Kanu-da, I hear you'll write my wedding poem?"[9]

The calamity must have been preordained, for precisely at that moment I was crossing out a few lines and adding new ones in their place in order to make the 'Best Wishes' more edifying. Keeping my eyes on the paper, I say, "Hm."

"Read out what you've written, let me hear."

I read, not without a touch of pride.

Sita, Savitri, Damayanti;[10] a woman's duties towards the motherland, towards her superiors such as the father-in-law, mother-in-law, husband etc.; and towards brothers-in-law, sisters-in-law, servants, the entire mankind and domestic animals—nothing has been left out in my poem; and I've concluded my 'Best Wishes' with a humble entreaty to God to shower His mercy and blessings on the heads of these newlyweds about to enter the unfamiliar and hazardous jungle of worldly life.

Having finished reading, as I'm putting down the paper on the table with great fondness, Ranu snatches it away and runs off. When I enter Ranu's house, shouting and pursuing the 'Best Wishes', she's coming out of their kitchen.

"Give me my paper," I cry. Ranu raises a finger, pointing into the interior of the kitchen and disappears.

Ranu's mother asks from inside the kitchen, "What is it, Kanu?"

I say, "I wrote a 'Best Wishes', Ranu's run away with it."

"O dear, so that's what she threw into the fire? Never seen such a pest of a girl in my life..."

I come away fighting back my tears. My whole body burns in terrible rage. I am not one bit sad that I won't be able to print and distribute the 'Best Wishes' with my name on it. What causes me unbearable feelings of hurt and indignation is that she has destroyed, so pointlessly and brutally, my composition, the fruit of so much labour and thought. It took me all of seven days to put together the poem. How many times did I correct it, how many times did I copy it before I could bring it up to my liking! How many times did I rack my brains to giddiness...I wasn't satisfied even after reading it two hundred times...And that poem she's thrown into the fire! This is the first time I dug out words from my own head, set them to metre and composed a poem. What a thing she's done to the first offspring of my muse! Thrown it into the blazing stove! I burn in the hell-fire of grief.

The *shehnais* are playing. Today is Ranu's wedding day. The other day, the comparison of Ranu to a king's treasure came to my mind by accident. Today it is pricking somewhere with a pang of wistfulness.

Draping the *ghomta*[11] over her head, Ranu goes away to her in-laws' house. Packing my trunks and bedding, I go away to Calcutta for my studies.

Ranu visits her parents' home; I, too, come home; but nothing worth mentioning happens.

The day it does happen, I am suddenly deluged with swiftly rushing waves of an exquisite, unfamiliar and glorious sensation—just as a dried-up river fills up in no time with floodwaters. I don't know when Eros awoke from slumber and started peeping in with his springtime spell; but now, there he stands, having thrown open the gates. And at once, to my exultant eyes, all land, water and sky become suffused with a rosy enchantment.

Ranu hasn't noticed me. I'm gazing at her blazing beauty and rampant maturity. Such a maniacal visual orgy is not a thing of everyday life. My eyes refuse to blink. It's happening right in our home…

At last, as soon as our eyes chance to meet, Ranu blushes and hastily leaves the place. My heart's vicious thirst begins to surge in my breast like waves of lava. Ranu's age is fourteen. But already at this age, thanks to her prodigious health, she has outgrown adolescence and reached the high noon of full maturity.

Just two days later, I meet her in the passage between the two houses. Spotting me from a distance, she stops short, as though to turn back. But instead, covering her face with her sari-end, she steps aside from the way and stands! While passing by, the words I say are, "I'm Kanu", but the turmoil that is raging inside my mind is the very image of a storm-ravaged sea. Ranu says, "That I know, and you're not fit to see my face,"[12] and she moves ahead with hurried steps. Following the chain of events, I understand well enough the meaning of her words but, though stung, cannot summon up a reproach. In the storm that has been aroused in my breast ever since I saw her with new eyes, resentment and reproach could do precious little to rear their heads!

I look at the floodlit rostrum within my heart. There, only she and I, like two lonely planets.

Ranu doesn't know so much.

Ranu returns to her husband's house.

Mrityu[13] suddenly appears a few days later and, lifting men and women to his mouth with both hands, seems to relentlessly devour them like a ravenous monster. The sky fills with wails and chants of "*Hari Bol*"[14]—"*Hari Bol*" in funeral processions, "*Hari Bol*" by the sick bed, "*Hari Bol*" at gatherings of people. But Hari pays no heed whatsoever to the frantic invocations of the terrified creatures. People keep dying.

On the seventh day of the epidemic, Ranu's parents meet their doom within twelve hours of each other. Sending the bad news to Ranu, we flee.

We have returned. In six months, the graveyard has turned into a human habitation again.

Father writes to Ranu to make some arrangement for their house. Ranu writes back, "Sell it off, please." That day, I, too, receive a letter. Just one look, and I know the address has been written by Ranu.

She's written:

> *Kanu-da,*
>
> *The greatest sorrow of my life is that I will never again meet you in life.*
>
> *Do you remember those two days? The day you didn't eat the food I gave you in anger, and the day I threw your 'Best Wishes' poem into the fire? You don't know the reason, of course. Know just this: I couldn't stand your glee.*
>
> *You are a brahmin, I am a shudra;*[15] *please accept my pranam.*[16]
>
> *Ranu.*

After reading Ranu's letter, I remain gazing into space. My eyes don't blink. My mind is lost in amazement.

But I was fated to meet her again. Her husband gets transferred to our town and rents the very house of hers that was sold off.

After the initial crying and tears, once she has settled down in her friendship with my wife, I find she's drawn Indira into the closest intimacy, and banished me entirely from her domain. I hoped she would at least come to take my foot-dust,[17] greeting me as Kanu-da, but she doesn't.

"Ranu's son has turned out so good-looking," says Indira.

"Ought to; they're both good-looking."

'She's offered to give me the boy."[18]

It wouldn't have been unnatural for Indira to ask for the boy. I say, "You asked, perhaps?"

"No, no, why should I ask? She herself said: 'Sister, you take my son.'"

"Very compassionate, I'm sure."

Indira suddenly blushes. This charming bashfulness of hers reminds me that my last words might have a very far-reaching meaning. Unless Indira's hopes of motherhood have been totally given up, there can be no question of compassion in Ranu's offer. But Indira's age is only fifteen.

I ask, "What's the boy's name?"

"Benu."

In my mind I recite, "Kanu–Benu."[19] I don't know why, but a deep, hidden meaning and motive behind naming the boy "Benu" and making a mock offer in order to put him into my arms by a pseudonymous transaction seems to slowly become clear.[20] Maybe my imaginings are baseless, maybe thought and wish are just inseparable from each other, but still I savour, with utmost satisfaction, the pleasurable thrill, born of a delusion, that runs through my heart. Limits are crossed without any inhibition whatsoever.

Looking at Benu's face, Indira says, "Two teeny pearly teeth. Want to take him?"

"Give." Benu freely comes into my outstretched arms.

Indira smiles and says, "Quite friendly."

The words enter my ears, but my mind is then racing away in a different direction. This baby…born of her body…the embodiment of the satisfaction of her most intimate desire. It's her throbbing life, her blood secreted drop by drop from her body, the joyous sap of her heart that, transported, is touching my body…

Raising my face, I see Indira gazing at Benu with terribly hankering eyes. As soon as I raise my eyes, Indira gives a slight smile and moves away. There's hankering in my eyes, too. But the two are as unlike as smile and tears.

I look at Benu's eyes. These are exactly like those. Where the differences are and where not, where likeness meets unlikeness—my vision, transcending all such analysis in an instant, sinks in the azure ocean of their vision.

Suddenly I feel incomplete. Half of my life, detached and displaced from its orbit, has set me adrift. There's unity and peace everywhere. Only my restless, overheated fantasies about what might have happened if something else were to happen have left one part of me parched and aching; but in the other part there's also a boundless, palpitating fear, lest one day this pain be dulled and my mind fall into a despondent, decrepit inertia.

Coming back, Indira becomes frantic: "Is that the way to hold a baby?"

I put Benu back into her hands and say, "Will get the hang of it by and by. No harm if somebody else's baby suffers a little discomfort until then." I get a rebuke.

Jealousy becomes the enemy of my clandestine pleasure. The experience of my own conjugal life makes my heart ache by repeatedly calling up an image: Ranu as another man's wife. This sensation is not something to be nursed in the mind happily, fondly, and at ease. Its inexorable lance-thrusts seem to drive me crazy.

Indira brings a fresh piece of news: "This Ranu's a loony."

"Meaning?"

"Says, 'Come, missus,[21] you and I—let's become one.'"

"Sign of a loony surely. What did you say?" I ask, and she gives some reply, too, but by then Indira in her audible and palpable reality has been completely obliterated for me. Raging flames of ecstasy ignite my nerves and veins, and set my hairs on end all over the body in a riotous celebration.

I don't know how long I remain entranced in the surging ecstasy or what I have been doing. When I come round, I see Indira staring at me in amazement. Managing a slight smile, I say, "What's it I was saying?" Indira says, "You said nothing. *I* was saying that…" She stops abruptly and gets up. I grab her hand and say, "Why do you go? Why so angry suddenly?"

"Not angry; only it's a bother to talk to an absent-minded man like you."

"Okay, forgive me this once. Ranu said something like a loony. What did you say to that?"

Indira alone knows how she takes the whole thing, but says in a normal enough tone, "I told her, 'Be so if you can, but then someone will have to give up his missus.' Ranu said, 'Ask Kanu-da if he's ready to give up his.'"

"No way." I am about to raise my arms to hug her but stop and say, "An arrangement of sorts could be made if one could come to an understanding with Basanta Babu."

But Indira's interest seems put out abruptly.

Six months have passed.

Basanta Babu's transfer order has arrived by wire.

All these days I haven't come face to face with Ranu. She hasn't come to our house. "Too much bother, dear; can't chat properly," she's told Indira and called her away.

The day before the departure, Ranu comes to our house. She puts the baby in Indira's arms and, after doing a pranam at my feet, says, "Kanu-da, we're leaving tomorrow. Your missus will sleep with me tonight.[22] Such a good girl, your missus."

"Good girl, indeed," I say and, not being able to decide whether to smile at Ranu or at Indira, I smile at my law books.

"Agreed?"

From the way I start, I realise my mind was wandering.

"To what?"

"Just like him," says Indira. "Always absent-minded."

Ranu says, "I was saying your missus will sleep with me tonight. Won't meet again..." Her voice sounded thick.

I say, "Okay."

"Just as I said," says Indira.

"What?"

"This Ranu's a loony."

"What's she said now?"

After a brief silence Indira says, "Who'd have known…" and then stops short and goes on laughing a lot.

I wait in silence. When she stops laughing, I ask, "What is it?"

"As if husband and wife," says Indira, "she and I."

I smother a sigh. She's wiped my touches clean off Indira's body and carried them away, saturating her skin and blood with them.

I am satisfied.

Notes

1. 'Kanu' is a diminutive of Krishna, the lover-god (see note 3, 'A Bond Defiled'; and for '*da*', see note 7, 'Son and Son's Wife').

2. Perhaps the most famous Bengali sweet, made by soaking balls of the solid part of curdled milk in syrup.

3. See page *xvi* of the 'Introduction' concerning the ages of the characters.

4. A common way of addressing and referring to a daughter, daughter-in-law, and also women in general in Bengal, now going out of vogue.

5. See note 14, 'Son and Son's Wife'.

6. A red dye made of lac, part of the traditional daily toilet of Bengali women.

7. See note 1, 'Son and Son's Wife'.

8. Because she is now pledged to another man.

9. A quaint Bengali custom, now almost extinct. Verses ranging from didactic to humorous and entitled 'Best Wishes' or something similar, written by a local talent who was often a close relative or friend, would be printed in coloured ink on superfine paper to be distributed among the wedding guests.

10. Three model women of epic and mythology.

11. See note 15, 'So Long as the Sun and Moon'.

12. One reason can be that he was leering at her, now another man's wife. But the reason may also be that he has not been man enough.

13. The god of death. Here it alludes to an epidemic, like cholera or bubonic plague, which frequently broke out in those days.

14. An invocation of the god Hari, another name for Krishna.

15. The lowest of the four Hindu castes.

16. Obeisance; see note 6, 'So Long as the Sun and Moon'. A brahmin may not marry a shudra, nor, strictly, accept food from one, but does accept a shudra's pranam. In this first avowal of her feelings for Kanu, she seems to suggest that Kanu refused the food and gloated over her marriage because he is a brahmin and she a shudra. This is not true, of course, and she surely knows it herself. But she would have every right to suspect that, because of this caste difference, Kanu would not have agreed to marry her and was just angling for a dalliance—a suspicion she cannot voice directly.

17. See note 6, 'So Long as the Sun and Moon'.

18. Not literally, of course. It is a purely formulaic expression of friendship between two mothers. A little later Kanu makes the mistake of interpreting it as an expression of Ranu's compassion.

19. 'Kanu' is Krishna and 'Benu' means flute, the two being inseparable. Krishna plays the flute to charm the lovelorn Radha (see note 3, 'A Bond Defiled').

20. A rather abstruse sentence bearing testimony to Jagadish Gupta's prolonged proximity to legal sound and fury. But the general meaning seems clear: Kanu thinks that in the name of offering the boy to Indira, Ranu was actually offering the boy to him.

21. In the original, the word used by Ranu for 'missus' on this page and the next is '*bou*'. This Bengali word can be variously used to mean or address a wife (one's own or somebody else's), brother's wife, and often loosely to mean or address any younger married woman (and several others not relevant here). With great subtlety, Jagadish Gupta makes Ranu use the word '*bou*' in *all these senses*, and it is hoped 'missus' more or less covers this range. Incidentally, among the educated classes in Bengal, to which the characters of this story belong, it is common to refer to a wife as 'missus'.

22. A common enough practice among women friends, by itself with no deeper suggestion.

Mrs Havoc*

His two eyes are round and red; in length and breadth, he's humongous; but more fearful than his size and appearance is his speech.

Sodu Khan speaks very softly, in a hushed voice. The mismatch between his speech and his appearance is such that, hearing his words, one is forthwith reminded of a smoking fire.

As a matter of fact, his words are just like smoke—kind of light—and people, unable to figure out when the tongues of fire will flick out from inside, crumple up completely before him. The few who are his favoured men exercise not a little power as Sodu's men, but before him they, too, remain shrivelled up, like toads in winter.

Previously, Sodu used to do *gaonwaal*, that is, peddle from village to village, carrying on his head such knick-knacks as waist-cords, copper amulets, balls of thread, needles, tin-framed mirrors, wooden boxes, toys, etc.

Then he started working as a *phorey*—scouring the villages to collect ten or twenty *seer*[1] of such seasonal harvests as jute,

*Originally published in Bengali as *'Pralayankari Shashthi'*, in 1927.

linseed, mustard, *rai*,[2] rice, coriander, wheat, sesame, lentil, etc., and supplying these to the wholesaler.

Then he became a *byapaari*, that is to say, when a merchant's boat went to the trading-station loaded with jute or rice, Sodu Khan would travel up and down with it, taking charge of the boat and the cargo.

Presently, buying a thousand-*maund*[3] sail-boat, he himself becomes a merchant and sits in office.

Lucky man—his fortune turns around rapidly. Money keeps pouring freely into his hands. But the man's skulduggery remains.

He goes to the market, grabs and lifts the best fish by the snout and pointlessly asks, "How much?"

"Two-and-a-half rupees,"[4] says the fishmonger.

"Two-and-a-half? Rather cheap!" Sodu says, and hands the fish to his servant.

Any outsiders there would imagine perhaps it's truly cheap to Sodu, but those who know him smile to themselves; the fishmonger quails.

While departing, Sodu tosses a half-rupee coin into the fishmonger's basket and leaves. The fishmonger tucks in at his waist whatever has been salvaged.

The other day, the moneylender Nidhiram Datta's house caught fire. Such things happen quite often. In the village, this, too, is a small-time trade. For throwing a lighted match on the thatch, whether or not it starts a fire, the fee is one rupee. For poking smouldering charcoal into a haystack, it's three rupees. For setting fire to all four corners of a house, it's five rupees. For setting fire after bolting the door from outside, so that the people inside can't come out, it's ten rupees. Sodu Khan used to be the don of all this.

But meanwhile, he's made a name as a big trader far and wide. He has three boats. His goods are bought and sold from Dhaka on one side, to Rajmahal on another side, to Calcutta on yet another. A two-storeyed building has come up as well, with twenty rooms. A drawing-room, carpets, cushions, long-piped hookahs, short-piped hookahs, scented tobacco, brass pitchers—everything has been acquired. Wage-maids, bond-maids, table-boys—even these are no fewer than ten or twenty. Wives have been found, too—five or so—nearly half-a-dozen. All the wives have separate apartments, and each has two personal bond-maids.

Wage-maids, bond-maids, wives. Sons and daughters are being born of them all. In just three or four years such a large house of Sodu Khan has come to beat even a congeries of wild pigeons in filth and din.

From each boat-trip, Sodu rakes in four or five thousand rupees. Yet he's never given up one habit of his: always he must go on one or the other of the boats. Now this one, then another—in this way he travels on all three boats by turns, accompanied by two or so wage-maids or bond-maids, as well as his weighing clerk, Chaitanya. Such an awesome, seasoned chap as Chaitanya isn't easily found. With the scales he can swing in up to a seer-and-a-half at a time—such a clean pair of hands he has.

Sodu's boat is moored at the *ghat* of Kaliganj bazaar. Bales of jute, after being unloaded and weighed at the ghat itself, are going up into the merchant's warehouse.

A little to the north of the bazaar-ghat is the bathing-ghat. Perched on the boat's shed with an umbrella over his head and watching the loading and unloading of the cargo, Sodu suddenly looks towards the bathing-ghat and thinks, "Aha, a nice little wifey, I say!"

A married woman of twenty or twenty-two has come to fetch water and, slightly lifting her *ghomta*,[5] is watching the weighing of Sodu's jute bales. Sodu summons one of the two bond-maids who've come with him to do the cooking, and sets her on the trail of the woman. The maid locates the woman's house and secretly points it out to Sodu.

The following day, Sodu, taking a walk, lands up at the house just next to it. As soon as he stands in the outer yard, the people of the house warmly ask him in and give him a stool to sit on. They know Sodu by face as a big merchant and a respectable man, so they cordially offer him betel and hubble-bubble. But Sodu is scarcely able to have a proper smoke. As he puffs at the hubble-bubble, tears suddenly come rolling down his cheeks in a continuous stream. The people of the house are astonished.

They ask, "Why're you crying?"

Sodu says, "I'm crying in great sorrow, brothers. By Allah's grace I've seen the one I never hoped to see."

Everyone's jaw drops.

Sodu goes on, "I've seen the very one, brothers. It's my sister. A married girl was taking water from the bathing-ghat... Suddenly, as I looked at her, my heart missed a beat. Who's it I'm seeing! Exactly my dead sister, as if returned from heaven. Same features, same figure, even the walk exactly like her. It's she, absolutely." So saying Sodu drops the hubble-bubble and starts crying even more.

Somebody says, "Jasim's wife, of that house. It's she, so pretty."

So much for the day. Sodu comes away after a good deal of crying.

But almost at once, word reaches the ears of Jasim and his folks. They go and meet Sodu in his boat and say, "Please drop by once to sit a while in our humble house."

The next day, Sodu turns up at Jasim's house with two hampers of crispy *batasa* and *jilapi*.[6] He is received and entertained appropriately—as a brother visiting a sister's house should be.

Taking the sister's son in his lap, Sodu can hardly let go—such is the attachment. He talks about his sister's childhood and about her growing up, and praises her profusely.

After treating the neighbourhood people to another four or five hampers of batasa and jilapi on his nephew's account, Sodu goes away from the place with his boat.

About fifteen days later, Sodu's man comes to Jasim's house with clothes worth about a hundred rupees. Clothes and handkerchiefs for the sister; clothes, shoes and a red umbrella for the nephew; clothes, shoes, towels and umbrellas for Jasim and his two brothers; plus sweets of umpteen kinds. With these comes a letter—day and night his heart is pining away for his sister.

It sets off a regular hubbub in Jasim's house. How to contain the glee! So much—all this—ours—for keeps!

People begin to say, "Well, now Jasim's found a brother-in-law, his misery's over at long last. Won't have to mow jute any more, standing in waist-high water."

However, something must be given in return for so much received, if only to save face. But the plight of Jasim's family is hand-to-mouth; nothing but some five seer of batasa is sent with great difficulty. Yet this leaves them no room for regret. The sentiments Sodu conveys, having received just those five seer of batasa, are such as if he'd come upon the open pit of a goldmine.

As the exchanges of cordiality continue in this manner, suddenly one day a wedding, somehow or other, becomes imminent in Sodu's house. Sodu's messenger comes to Jasim's house with a letter, and an eight-bearer palanquin, a couple of escorts and a maidservant come to fetch the sister.

The letter reads:

> *Brother Jasim,*
>
> *My younger brother's wedding is on the __th. Send my sister without fail. Eight days are left for the wedding. You all must set out a day or two in advance and come. Do not decline or refuse...*

Jasim's wife rides in the palanquin, escorts and messenger with their pikes and the staffs before and behind, and arrives at Sodu's house to the accompaniment of the "*Hoom*! *Hoom*!"

of the bearers. Jasim's younger brother Kasem—a lad of fifteen or sixteen—also comes with her. The palanquin goes in and is lowered directly at the door of the inner apartments, and Jasim's wife goes inside with the maid.

Three days before the marriage is due, Sodu calls Kasem aside and says, "The marriage won't take place on this date. I'm giving a man with you, go home for now. Tell Brother Jasim they'll definitely get the news before the marriage."

Kasem says, "And Sister?"

"Sister will stay here for a few days. I'll make arrangements for her later."

Kasem goes away.

Before long, Jasim and the others become rather concerned about his wife. That apart, however much the intimacy and kinship, it doesn't look nice to go and stay so long in someone else's house.

At last Jasim skips a day's work to come to Sodu's house.

Sitting in the veranda outside Sodu's drawing-room, Jasim is musing, "Good Lord, what a big house!"—when the master of the house comes in, and he stands up. Complacently, Jasim gives a little smile, too, but Sodu raises his brows and says, "What d'you want?" Sodu's manner is offhand, as if he doesn't even know Jasim.

Jasim thinks maybe big folks do make such jests. So he smiles a little more and says, "You don't recognise me, Brother?"

"No, man, no. Who're you? Where's your home?"

At Sodu's temper, it occurs to Jasim that this mightn't be a rich man's jest after all. He's astounded. Pausing a moment to compose himself, he says, "But your name is Sodu Khan?"

"Yes, my name's Sodu Khan."

"Then I don't understand why you can't recognise me. My name is Jasim Karigar;[7] my house is at Kaliganj."

Sodu says, "I know Kaliganj sure enough. Been there a few times. But you I don't know. To hell with that—now why are you here?"

Jasim says, "My wife..."

"Ran away, is it?"

Jasim listens and is all at sea. After gaping blankly for some time at Sodu's face, he timidly says, "You brought her…"

Abruptly Sodu lets out a roar like a tiger, "Jendaar!"

"Sir," responds his servant Jendaar, and, tossing his shaggy mane around, comes up and stands there. As soon as Jasim sees him, even the little strength that was left in his arms and legs after reaping jute in waist-high water gives out. As he looks at Jendaar's oil-smeared body, jet-black like a bumble-bee's, his tongue moves slightly in his throat to make a hiccup-like sound: "Allah Huq."[8]

Sodu raises a finger at Jasim and says, "The bugger's mad. Says I've brought away his wife. Chop off the whoreson's ears and pack him off across the river."

As Jendaar comes up, saying, "Yes, sir", Jasim breaks into sobs. Folding his hands, he says, "Please, sir, I'm your son, please save me."

Sodu says, "Go then, don't be mad again."

Who knows how he gets the tip, but Jasim comes and throws himself before just the right person.

Arjun is a *namashudra*,[9] an old man of seventy. After hearing everything, he says, "Go to the police station. What can we do?"

But Jasim would have none of it. Over and over again, he keeps saying the same thing: "You people go to Sodu just once. You only have to tell him, and he'll let go of my wife." The poor fellow doesn't yet know that Sodu has already married his wife and has been living in her apartment. He keeps crying and trying to fall at Arjun's feet.

Arjun says, "Let's go and see. But the matter won't be easy to settle. You don't know him."

Seeing Arjun with Jasim, Sodu smiles and says, "So, my boy Ram? Brought Hanuman[10] with you?"

These are his first words. Then a lot of words are bandied between the two sides, amounting very much to an altercation. Sodu doesn't say Jasim's wife is not in his house, nor does he say she is. Dodging the point, he just keeps blustering at them: "Whatever it is between us, two Muslims, who the hell are you to butt in?"

Jasim doesn't speak a word in fear.

Presently it's Sodu who has the last word. Taking a dig at their caste, he says, "You people see reason only after getting a shoe-thrashing. Had no shoe on your pates for a long time, eh?"

Arjun's eldest nephew, Judhishthir, has one look at Arjun's face and drags him out, shouting: "This scrap will be settled by the stick. Let us know when you want it."

Sodu, too, shouts back: "Okay."

Both sides know a fight is inevitable.

There are about twenty-five[11] in Judhishthir's party. All are Arjun's disciples. Some more people could have been found, if sent for. But Arjun doesn't allow it. "They're no more than two hundred, after all", he says. The only outsiders in the party are Jasim and his two brothers. Even they are just spectators. Not allowed to wield sticks.

The field adjoining the namashudra village used for grazing cattle is chosen as the venue for the fight. Sodu himself has proposed it. Perhaps his intention is to beat these people back into their homes and, in the same drive, raze their houses as well. Judhishthir once raises an objection, but Arjun says, "No, there it'll be."

A day is fixed.

On the appointed day, they come. They must surely number two hundred, maybe more, not less.

On this side, only twenty-two. Invincible, controlled power in every inch of their upright bodies, sturdy as twenty-two finely built bulls. No inhibition anywhere from head to foot. Each wears a *rudraksha*[12] rosary around the neck, a red dhoti, and a vermilion spot on the forehead,[13] and carries a four-cubit-long stick in hand.

Gathering them all, Arjun says, "You advance very slowly. I'm coming." And immediately he enters his house. There he sits tight on the ground for some five minutes with his eyes shut. Then, as he stands up, opening his eyes and bellowing "Ma! Ma!", his earlier appearance has been totally transformed—he's now as if Shiva the Annihilator incarnate.[14]

Then he comes out. Usually he's so doddery he's hardly able to walk. But now he rushes on, as if at the scent of blood. His roar could make a tiger's heart tremble—such is the fire in his voice! On the crests and troughs of his rippling, iron-hard muscles, in their movements of contraction and expansion, dances Rudra's[15] fury.

Chanting "Ma! Ma!", Arjun rushes up and says, "Come along!" and at once with a roar charges into the field.

What transpires next we can't describe very well.

Some hurricanes come on in this manner. You only hear the rush of the wind. Your eyes suddenly close in the gloom. As you open your eyes you see a few dismembered humans lying about, the rest all desolation. A similar cataclysm is over in a flash.

When the fight comes to an end, all these twenty-two feel as if they have come back to earth after ages. In the field, there is no one except Arjun and his men. Jasim and his two brothers are standing at a distance, trembling all over.

Jasim does not get back his wife. She herself refused to come.[16]

Notes

1. Slightly less than a kilogram.
2. A variety of mustard.
3. Something like forty tonnes.

4. In today's terms, perhaps four to five hundred rupees.

5. See note 15, 'So Long as the Sun and Moon'.

6. Cheap sweets. See note 7, 'A Primal Issue'.

7. The literal meaning of the surname is 'artisan', indicating a person of humble birth in the formally casteless Muslim society.

8. The meaning, apparently, is something like 'Allah the Just'. That the invocation, the very sound of which seems to stick in the throat, made by the victim remains unanswered is characteristic of Jagadish Gupta.

9. A lowly Hindu caste, the people of which are, however, extremely independent, proud and militant.

10. The mythological Monkey God, immensely powerful and loyal helper of Ram, the hero of the epic *Ramayana*. Ravan, king of the Rakshasas, stole Ram's wife Sita, just as Sodu has stolen Jasim's wife. With the help of Hanuman and an army of lesser monkeys, Ram defeated Ravan and rescued Sita. The irony of course is that Jasim is anything but a hero!

11. A little later the number is given as twenty-two, presumably after excluding Jasim and his brothers.

12. A kind of dried fruit used as beads for a rosary.

13. The way they have turned out for the fight bespeaks a tantric blood-rite. In tantra, the motive power of the universe is believed to be feminine. Goddess Durga, 'saviour of the distressed', represents its benign aspect while Kali, the fearful goddess of massacre whom Arjun invokes a little later with "Ma! Ma!" is its other aspect. Every woman is an embodiment of this primeval energy. She can do immense good but, if treated wrongly, can turn into a Mrs Havoc.

14. Supernatural agency or just auto-suggestion? All we can say is that this part of the story has a striking similarity to a story by the celebrated author Pramatha Chaudhury, who at least was noted for his rational and cerebral approach.

15. The manifestation of Shiva as The Destroyer.

16. We are left to recall that Ram did get back his wife (Note 10), then repeatedly doubted and shamed her for being a victim of abduction, and finally banished her to stop the wagging tongues of society and maintain his family's honour.

The Eighteenth Art*

Benukar Mandal, resident of Nachansaha village, has a few *bigha*[1] of land, a plough for tilling the land, and bullocks for drawing the plough. He has some dues to collect from a few, some dues to pay up to others, and a little unploughed land adjoining his house where the previous day's ash from the *unoon*[2] is dumped. The piled up ash is spread out and the soil is dug up for growing herbs; this one little pleasure he has.

Besides these, he has his wife, Janaki, and he has a discontent in his mind. No one else, nothing else.

Benukar has some looks, of course, though nothing great; and some wits, though none too sharp. But he doesn't make mistakes in farming and reckoning up his accounts.

And it is also worth mentioning that he does have one fault—he doesn't wake at dawn, but after the sun is up.

Benukar's age is just about twenty-six; his wife Janaki's just about nineteen. It's four years they've been married.

Four years of married life is not a short time. Moment by moment, very slowly, time is wearing on.

*Originally published in Bengali as '*Atharo Kalar Ekti*', date unknown.

Hence it might be expected that some order has come to Benukar's notions of gratification, and some sobriety to his desire. People do expect of people such composure and contentment when they find that four years of married life have been lived through, and life has settled down to a plain, workaday state and attained a tranquillity in its external aspect. They expect this of others, though their own plight their minds know. People make—are compelled to make—the mistake of expecting the same of themselves, too, taking the ennui and inertia of domesticity for temperance, but what can keep their minds from restlessly fidgeting in silence inside! As a matter of fact, Benukar Mandal does remain restless, and there's a discontent in his mind.

In tracing the source of Benukar's discontent, one mustn't forget the dire truth: that they've been married for four years, and four years is an extremely long time for short-lived humans. Hence, if the wife's figure and gestures keep growing passé to the eye as a result of the relentless togetherness of these extremely long four years, how can one help it! Man seeks but can't find a way to prevent it. This irremediable situation creates a tremendous discontent—as it has done in Benukar's case.

Janaki's age is just about nineteen. During the four years since the time she was fifteen, she, as Benukar's round-the-clock helpmate in all things, has pervaded Benukar's life not only at the level of the mind, but also in practical work. By providing empathy and cooperation in farming, caring for bullocks and growing vegetables, she has won Benukar's admiration.

Yet Benukar might be forgiven if his fifteen-year-old wife feels, four years later, at the age of nineteen, a trifle dimmed and distant to him precisely on account of such relentless cooperation. This need not be transgression of a singularly perverted mind. The reason for this is simply that all humans are, by nature, impious in their heart of hearts, and neurosis resides within every one of them. The time that has passed, since the taking of the first step when she was fifteen until now when she's nineteen, has worn away their lifespan, given them a few things and robbed them of others—Benukar doesn't care. But it has vitiated his drink with an unknown adulterant—it's this that is most terrible, and this has produced the discontent in his mind. A terrible thing, this discontent, for humans. If it didn't arise, then youth would have no need for ever-new adornments and embellishments, and the artistry of the side-glance would have become extinct. Moreover, the unbridled youthfulness that for four years has appeared to Benukar as a power uniquely Janaki's own, as her tethering art, now no longer appears to be so. It's been mentioned that there's a discontent in Benukar's mind; here's the source of that discontent. Janaki's ruby lips and white teeth are lovely as before, the fullness of her body is still unexhausted—but that's about all. There aren't any further inventions, by way of what could be named playfulness, that would constantly renew her, so that Benukar's temptation, affection and craving and, finally, satisfaction, would know no limits.

Ultimately what it boils down to is that Benukar Mandal—peasant, householder, owner of a plough and bullocks—is craving to witness a creative play of his wife's mind, a cycle of metamorphoses, a resurgence of savour after savour. "Damn it," he thinks, "so boring, tired of it all."

Janaki is a splendid cook, and just as neat and smart at finishing her work fast. She knows everything—from the delicate needlework for mending torn clothes to pedalling the *dhenki*[3] to make rice and *chinra*.[4] But she doesn't know that her distinctiveness and worth as an entity has depreciated a little.

This suddenly becomes known today.

After sweeping the rooms and lighting the evening lamp,[5] a housewife has no work in hand for a while. Conches and bells are then sounded all around. When men were savage and hadn't learnt to protect their dwellings, the evenings looked terrible for fear of wild beasts and there was a need to produce such plentiful metallic din, but now these are sounded in temples, at the time of *arati*.[6] Be that as it may, the time is one of repose.

In Benukar's house, there's a pause in work at such a time. He's sitting engrossed in puffing at his hubble-bubble; Janaki is sitting close by, legs stretched out. Both are silent. While puffing at his hubble-bubble at this gloomy but auspicious hour, Benukar suddenly feels as if the immense fullness that was in the flavour of life's nectar is no more; his thirst isn't being quenched quite to the end—as if someone has poured water into his drink. His aforementioned discontent suddenly awakens with full force.

Benukar stops puffing at his hubble-bubble and looks at the sky. There's nothing there, and his eyes see nothing. When the oil dries up and the lamp's flame is about to go out, a mute wailing rises up from somewhere—it's not clear whether it's from the mind or from the flame. There's a similar sad gloom of defeated impotence in the sky. Benukar doesn't have eyes sensible of the reflection of the colours, messages and movements of the sky; still, he stares open-mouthed at the sky for some time. Then he lowers his eyes and looks at his wife, Janaki. And looking at her, he gives a little, wan smile—as if he is trying to cover up some anxiety.

Janaki has noticed the up-and-down movement of her husband's eyes. "What?" she asks.

"Nothing," says Benukar, "but just wanted to ask something."

Sweetly Janaki says, "Go ahead, let's hear."

Benukar again smiles a little; his smile, he fancies, is smoothing the path for his subsequent words. Then he says, "I hear a woman has eighteen arts—is it true?"

Janaki instantly understands what her interlocutor means to say. She says, "Not true. Not eighteen, but a lot more. Some say thirty-six, others say fifty-four." Apparently, Janaki hasn't forgotten the tables she once memorised till twenty.

Benukar is amazed. Taking a few more puffs at the hubble-bubble, he says, "So many? But I see not even one of them in you!"

"No great wonder! I don't show, so you don't see."

Benukar keeps silent. If a person can show something but doesn't, one might beg them to show it; but a woman's arts are not things to be elicited by begging, whatever their number.

Janaki asks, "Whose tricks have you fallen for? Or has someone taught you to sing this tune?"

Benukar says, "Nothing like that. Just came to mind, so I asked."

"Want to see?"

Benukar now feels embarrassed. The matter turns awkward as soon as she offers to give what he's been inwardly missing and thirsting for. A gift that can be received as something priceless so long as the intention remains unspoken doesn't feel right if it's offered with an explicit statement. One can't even make out how it feels.

Benukar puts away his hubble-bubble and keeps his face lowered.

Janaki says, "Art—in a ploughman's shack! Okay, I'll show."

Benukar turns his face and goes away utterly abashed.

Baishakh[7] is drawing to a close. If the soil were soaked just a little by rain, the ploughing could be started, but there's not a trace of clouds. The lack of rain has become a matter of great worry, when one day God takes pity and in the afternoon the clouds discharge water with great sound and fury. The rain isn't plentiful but promising for a start. The farmers become jubilant—the fields can be ploughed now.

Benukar says, "So then, it's rained."

"Now leave me and love the bullocks," says Janaki.

Benukar says, "Tut!"

"Why 'tut'?" says Janaki, bringing a touch of bitterness into her voice. Then, hiding her thoughts, she says, "So to the field tomorrow?"

"Of course."

"Which field will you plough first?" Having cooperated with her husband body and soul for four years, she knows all their fields.

Benukar says, "The field on the east has three plots side by side—I'll do that first. It'll take two days. It slopes down south, so

I have to plough it from the north. But, no great hurry." Having planned out the ploughing, Benukar looks at the sky—clouds are drifting about.

Next day, not at dawn, but in the morning after the sun is up, Benukar has his *muri*,[8] *gur*[9] and water, and with great joy sets out for the field with his bullocks, plough, hubble-bubble, etc. Just then Janaki calls from behind and says, "Taken the matchbox?"

Benukar turns around and says, "Eh, calling back on the very first day!"

"Young wife calling back," says Janaki, "brings good luck."

Benukar says, "Tut!"

"Why 'tut'?" Then she adds, "Don't put the matchbox on the ground—it'll get soaked."

Benukar says, "Okay," and goes out.

But that day it isn't possible to plough more than two plots. The sun is too hot and there's no great need for hurry, too, in the excessive sun.

While eating, Benukar says, "The south plot is left. Tomorrow, once that's done, I'm through with this field."

The next day Benukar is to go to the field again, but before that—which means very early in the morning—Janaki is seen to leave bed; and she is then further seen running towards the eastern field with a bundle of rags and a sharp spud.

She isn't going on any farm work, to be sure, but on some other business...

In the morning, a little after sunrise, Benukar comes to plough the field, having taken muri, gur and water as before. After a sweltering night, the summer morning feels very soothing, and he happily yokes the bullocks to the plough. Brandishing the goad with a flourish, he steps down into the field from the boundary-ridge.

His bullocks understand his commands, and move and stop at his word. At his command, the bovine pair starts moving and drawing the plough. Slowly the plough moves along the sides of the rectangular field. Clods of the underlying dry soil, dug up and loosened by the force of the plough, seem to be sprouting up on the two sides of the furrow cut by the ploughshare. It is so satisfying to watch—as if something wonderful and new is being created. Benukar's farming zeal soars up.

But his farming zeal doesn't last. After his plough has gone around the four sides of the field twice and come midway of the third lap, Benukar looks at the upturned soil and is struck absolutely dumb with amazement. Until then the plough has been cutting and churning up the earth, but at this particular spot it has brought up not just the underlying soil, but something else as well from below the ground. From the half-cubit-long lump of soil on the ploughshare emerges—no flower, fruit, crop, snail, turtle-egg or treasure-trove—but a live *magur*[10] fish. Farmer Benukar Mandal forgets about farming, bullocks, plough, farmland, *dhaan*,[11] pulses, rain, Baishakh, shade and sun and all such, and remains staring fixedly at the magur fish. Wonderful apparition, this. The half-*seer*[12] fish—a denizen of water, but how vigorous and agile on land, too! It's trying to crawl along on its gills through the lumpy and powdered earth.

After he has gazed at the magur with unblinking eyes and gone through successive spells of astonishment, Benukar's mind is filled with boundless joy. This is called fate: when God wants to give, He'll even force it through your thatch.[13] It's a fact, but a still more beneficial fact is that when God wants to give, He'll even put a live magur in the soil. Just look, how the Lord of the Universe keeps track of even the daily meals of humble humans. What a miracle He's worked out of His affection so that the insignificant Benukar should eat!

Benukar leaves his plough, bullocks and hubble-bubble in the field. With the magur's head pinched between his fingers, and brimming over with gratitude to the Lord of the Universe, he runs home. Maybe Janaki is thinking of frying inedible summer aubergines and cooking some poppy-seed preparation and a sour broth of potato and pumpkin. None of these today. Today only magur soup and rice, nothing else. The hind part of a magur is even tastier than the front.

On the way he runs into Rajib Hazra. Rajib wishes to stand a while for a few words and ask why Benukar is running home with a soil-smeared magur fish in hand, but Benukar doesn't stop.

"Got by chance", he answers Rajib's questioning look and moves on at the same rapid pace.

Hearing the thumping of feet behind, Janaki straightens up holding the broom—she was sweeping the courtyard. She sees her husband has come home at an odd time, with a fresh magur fish in hand and a broad smile on face.

"Listen, what a marvel!" Beginning with this, Benukar tells her the history of how he has come by the fish. In the epilogue, he also says by way of the moral that when God wants to give, He'll even put a magur fish in dry earth—for the purpose of providing a meal...With even greater ecstasy, he then says, "There, take it. Nothing else today—soup of this fish and rice."

Janaki listens from first to last and then asks, "Where did you get the fish, dear? Lovely fish, I say!"

In reply, pouring endearment into his tone, Benukar says, "What did you hear then for so long! I was ploughing the field, and I suddenly found the fish had come up with the soil on the ploughshare"—and he looks on, goggle-eyed.

But, hearing this, Janaki says, "All lies!"

"All lies! Swear by you, swear by God!"

"Well then, put it in this bowl with some water."

With the deepest affection for each other, the husband and wife put the magur fish in a bowl of water to keep it alive for the time being. Getting water, the fish starts playing around and, looking at it, Benukar says, "Today I'll eat soup of this fish and rice. I'll come back early from the field." He turns to go to the field. Pausing at the door, he says, "Look at our luck."

Janaki says, "Mm."

Janaki has finished cooking early. Benukar, too, has returned early from the field. He says, "Going for my bath. Serve up."

Janaki says, "Okay, go."

In his eagerness for the magur soup, Benukar cannot enjoy his bath to the full. After two hasty dips in the pond, he gets up.

Hearing him return, Janaki asks, "Shall I serve?"

"Yes, yes, I'm changing my clothes."

After changing his wet clothes, Benukar comes and sits on the *pinri*[14] and says, "Now—bring."

Janaki serves rice on his plate and a broth in a bowl.

Looking at the broth, Benukar says, "Cooked *hinchey*[15] broth, too—why? You do like cooking."

Despite the praise, Janaki doesn't speak.

Benukar mixes a fourth of the rice with the leaf broth and eats it, having kept aside three-fourths of the rice for the magur soup. Then he says, "Now give the fish."

However amazed Benukar may have been at finding the magur fish in the soil of the field, he didn't quite lose his bearings. There was a limit to that amazement; it didn't muddle up his brain completely. But the amazement that is produced by Janaki's words when he asks for the fish is so great, it seems to exceed all limits, all yardsticks, all measures. Janaki distinctly says, "Where will I get a fish?"

Right from birth, Benukar doesn't understand banter. If he did, he might have taken the words as such and his head wouldn't have swum in such unbearable amazement.

Sitting bolt upright, he says, "Where will you get a fish? The fish I brought then—what's happened to it?"

"When did you bring a fish?"

"When did I bring? Didn't I bring a fish? Fed it to dogs and cats, have you?"

"Oh, come off it now. Let me give you some more leaf broth, eat up the rice. Don't be crazy ranting 'fish, fish'."

"'Crazy ranting fish, fish'? Dish out the fish soup, quick, I tell you, or it won't be good for you..." Benukar makes his eyes so red that before them any contradiction indeed seems out of the question.

Yet Janaki says, "What bad can you do after all, for no rhyme or reason?"

"What bad can I do after all, for no rhyme or reason? I'm still asking you gently—don't rile me too much."

"Where can I get a fish to cook soup for you? You've landed me in such a fix!"

"I've landed you in such a fix? Now see what a fix is." So saying Benukar has scarcely put out his grubby hand to grab Janaki's hair when, at this very trifling move of her husband, she lets out such a shriek of terror that Benukar himself draws back his hand with a start and stands up.

A lot of people live about the place. At the scream of a neighbourhood damsel in distress, three or four of them come rushing.

"Mandal, are you in? What's happened, Mandal-wife?" Elderly Nadhargopal[16] Choudhury asks from the courtyard and starts advancing.

Nadhargopal Choudhury was clerk to a pleader. Having once been thrashed for getting his fingers in the till, and once again for glowering even after failing to square the pleader's accounts, he has now settled down in the village. A son of Nadhar works as a salesman in a Calcutta shop. Frightfully complex matters of frightening law courts are all crystal clear to him. For this, and also because of his links to Calcutta sophistication via his son, he commands great respect in the village. He relishes nothing more than acting as the arbiter to settle disputes.

This Nadhar Choudhury questions Benukar and Janaki to know what the matter is.

But no reply comes from Benukar from inside the kitchen; the reply comes from Janaki. She says, "He rose to beat me for no reason."

"Why?" So saying Nadhar Choudhury et al. come up and stand in front of the kitchen.

Janaki draws the sari a little more over her head[17] and says, "Ask him and find out. Jabbering 'fish, fish', or some such rot."

Benukar says, "I'm jabbering 'fish, fish', or some such rot? Listen, Nadhar-*da*.[18] Early morning I went to plough the field. I've just done two rounds of ploughing when I see a magur fish—such a big magur, alive and kicking—has come up from the earth."

Nadhar Choudhury is elated at the complexity of the dispute. He says, "Aha! A magur fish from the earth! Then?" His look becomes piercing like a judge's.

The Plaintiff Benukar goes on, "I rush home. I say: 'Today I'll eat rice with the soup of this fish, cook it well.' And I pour water into a bowl and put the fish in it and go back to the field...After my bath I sit down to eat, and she serves only a hinchey broth... Wouldn't this make anyone angry?"

The Defendant Janaki says, "Heard him? Says he brought a fish!"

The Judge Nadhar Choudhury hears the complaint and defence of both parties and says, "Benu, dear brother, cool off. The water in the fields dried up in *Kartik*.[19] Now it's Baishakh. There can't be any magur fish in the earth, dead or alive."

"Can't be because you say so, I suppose! I found it, I took it, I carried it home by the hand, and here you act the councillor and declare simply on a guess there can't be."

Everyone starts laughing. "Gone off his head," says Kalipada.

Janaki says, "And because I didn't cook that fish soup, he rose to beat me."

"Of course, I'll beat you." As Benukar makes as if to charge again, Kalipada and others enter the kitchen and catch hold of him.

Nadhar Choudhury says, "Don't beat her for nothing, man! You didn't find a fish—why say such absurd things? This wouldn't wash in a court...Let me see your eyes." After looking into Benukar's eyes, Nadhar Choudhury says, "Turned red."

Gunamay Pal says, "Listen, Benukar, wash your hands and sit a while in a cool place—you'll get well in no time. If the Baishakh sun suddenly hits you in the head, it does play such tricks on the eye. Once it happened even to me. Just at midday I was returning from the field with my plough and two bullocks, but it seemed as if there weren't two bullocks, but four." While saying this, Gunamay himself brings water in a jug, washes Benukar's hands, and settles him in a cool place. "No fear, he'll be well," he tells Janaki.

Benukar is knocked all of a heap, completely crushed, almost in a coma by then.

Slumped on the veranda, head hung down, he waves his hand to say, "Go now you all."

The neighbours go out.

The leader of the do-gooders, Nadhar Choudhury, says before leaving, "We don't want to hear any more rows, take care."

Janaki keeps silent for a while. Then she smiles a little and says, "You wanted to see the eighteen arts, didn't you? This was one. Don't be angry—there, I'm touching your feet." So saying, Janaki literally touches her husband's feet and says, "I've made magur soup. Come eat."

Benukar gets up and goes to eat but doesn't speak a word in fury.

Notes

1. About a third of an acre.
2. A traditional wood- or coal-fired cooking stove made of clay or brick. Also known as *chulha* or *chula*.
3. See note 11, 'A Primal Issue'.
4. A widely used snack made from boiled, unhusked rice flattened and husked by a *dhenki*.
5. A daily ritual.
6. Ritual waving of a lamp for invoking a deity.
7. The first month of summer.

8. Another common snack made by parching rice on heated sand.

9. See note 10, 'A Primal Issue'.

10. A scale-less catfish that can breathe in air and so can survive for quite a while on land.

11. See note 8, 'A Primal Issue'.

12. See note 1, 'Mrs Havoc'.

13. A popular proverb.

14. A rectangular wooden board placed on the floor. Traditionally, in India, even a king would have his meal sitting on a pinri (a suitably grand one of course).

15. *Helencha*, a kind of water-cress.

16. The name refers to the plump baby-god Gopal; the word 'Nadhar' probably having the effect a nickname like 'dumpy' would have in English.

17. A demure gesture of modesty.

18. See note 7, 'Son and Son's Wife'.

19. A late autumn month. Six months have passed since.